The Singleton

by
Christina Tosin Fasoro

Edited by
Lindsay Morris

Copyright © 2017 Christina Tosin Fasoro

Unless otherwise indicated, all Scripture quotations are taken from the Holy Bible, New Living Translation, copyright ©1996, 2004, 2007 by Tyndale House Publishers, inc., Wheaton, Illinois 60189. All rights reserved.

All rights reserved, including the right to reproduce this book, or portions thereof in any form. No part of this text may be reproduced, transmitted, downloaded, decompiled, reverse engineered, or stored, in any form or introduced into any information storage and retrieval system, in any form or by any means, whether electronic or mechanical without the express written permission of the author.

The views expressed in this work are solely those of the author and do not necessarily reflect the views of the publisher, and the publisher hereby disclaims any responsibility for them.

ISBN: 978-1-326-89745-1

Cover design by Olivia Sualdea

Visit the author's website at:
www.Christinafasoro.co.uk

Dedication:

To the '*All My Friends Are Taken But I'm Still Single*' single; the '*I Can't Believe I'm Still Single*' single; the '*Pretend I don't Care*' single; the '*Happy & Content*' single; the '*Single Mother*'; the '*45 And Still Single*' single; the '*25 And Still Single*' single; the 'Divorcee'; the '*Promiscuous*' single; the '*No Ring, No Ting*' single; the '*Single Christian*'; the '*If I Don't Meet Bae At This Event...*' single; the '*I Trust God*' single; the '*I've Been Trusting God For A While Now*' single; the '*I'm Done Trusting God*' single; the '*Was Nearly Married*' single; the '*I Would Rather Be Single*' single and the '*I'm In A Relationship But......*' single? This book is dedicated to you! Yes YOU! Because you're very situation has provided me the content that fills these pages.

Table of Contents

Acknowledgements — vii

CHAPTER 1:
Say's The Woman Who Already Has A Man — 1
(Reasons why we struggle with being single.)

CHAPTER 2:
A Singleton's Struggle With Singleness — 31
(The Singleton: My story.)

CHAPTER 3:
What Next? — 45
(From struggle to contentment.)

CHAPTER 4:
How About You Heal First? — 87
(Healing from your past in preparation for your future.)

CHAPTER 5:
And In The Meantime? — 112
(While you 'wait' right? Wrong!)

CHAPTER 6:
Stay encouraged, you got this! — 123

About The Author

Christina to some and Tosin to others, *(although I do have a friend who can't make up her mind so just calls me Tosina!)* I am a woman on a mission and my mission is this: To share the Gospel of Jesus Christ openly, boldly and unapologetically using my life as a testimony. I'm proud to be a Singleton, but I'm also much more than that; I am a loving daughter, annoying sister, a loyal and witty *(if I do say so myself)* friend, and a believer of Jesus Christ. Besides writing, I love my job within Financial Crime, where I get to travel the world. I also love socialising with positive people, reading John Grisham novels and watching action movies while pigging out on junk food *(don't judge me!)*

Acknowledgements

My Saviour, Lord and Bestie, Jesus Christ
This book wouldn't even be possible if it wasn't for You, and I will be eternally grateful for bringing me out of the darkest time of my life and encouraging me to let my light shine. My entire lifetime still wouldn't be enough to say thank you, but I hope by being obedient in writing this book, it's a start to the gratitude and love I will always have for You. Thank You that even at my lowest, weakest, and ugliest, You wanted me.

Mummy
Against all odds, I'm still here! Knowing what you've been through in life, yet witnessing you continue to be the most humble and thankful person I know has motivated me to do the same. Your strength is not only to be admired, but also desired, and I hope you know just how much I love you and how much you inspire me.

Daddy John
To the first man on this earth that I have ever loved, thank you for loving me first! Thank you for giving me but a snippet of God's unconditional love for me and adopting me into your family like your very own. In spite of the difficulties you faced, I will always be grateful for the happy and stable childhood you and Mummy Micky provided me growing up and for the example of a great man, great father, and great husband you continue to be.

Laide & Ore:
I love you guys!!! (like for real, for real). You guys are the best sisters on earth I could have asked for, and your unwavering support and love for me (even at times when I didn't deserve

it) lets me know that no matter what, you guys have got my back!

Laide: Thank you for encouraging me to be different, that it's ok to be whoever God has made me to be, and for pushing me to chase my dreams; I want to be like you but still me when I grow up! I love you so much and I pray I continually make you proud.

Ore: Thank you for always making me laugh, for showing me that real friends are needed along the journey, and from the very beginning, thank you for welcoming me with open arms. I can be quite a handful (I know) but thank you for never having your hands too full for me.

Family & Friends:
You guys have been my rock, and words cannot explain how encouraging you all have been when I needed it the most. Thank you for your stern but loving words of advice when I was procrastinating with this book, and thank you for all your support and believing in me when all I had was an idea.

It wouldn't be right if I didn't acknowledge 3 people in particular, who embraced what God called me to do from the very beginning and supported me every step of the way.

(In Alphabetical order to cover my back☺)

Anita Okpor: Now you know outward affection of any kind just ain't our thing, but I have to let you know just how much of a great friend you are to me! My battles are your battles and your battles are mine. Thank you for taking on all the highs and lows of this book as if you were the one that wrote it. You truly are one of my biggest (and loudest) supporters.

David (silent 'N') Nwanegbu: When I first came to you years ago with my idea of writing a psychological thriller you said to me *'you can do anything you put your mind to Chris'* and believed in me even in my dark days, without Christ days. You and Theresa were the first 2 people I told about writing this book and you have supported me since day 1. You continuously push me closer to Christ and I will forever be grateful for our friendship.

Theresa Agonmuo: Theresa you continuously motivate me to be a better Christian, a better friend and a better person. You have been a Godsend in my life from the very beginning (*even though you claim we weren't friends* *rolls eyes*.) Thank you for relentlessly inviting me to church when I was broken; it paid off. I often catch a glimpse of you in service worshipping the Lord and to date; it is still the most beautiful, authentic and humbling sights my eyes have seen. I love you T!

Pastor Temi Odejide & House on the Rock London Family:
Last but certainly not least, I just want to acknowledge and say a massive thank you to my second home, House on The Rock London, and my spiritual father, Pastor Temi Odejide.

Pastor Temi, your weekly sermons have always encouraged me to keep chasing my dreams no matter the giants faced and to continually keep God at the centre of all I do. I want to thank you for being one of the causes of my spiritual growth and to let you know that your tenacity, diligence, and resilience in the face of adversity do not go unnoticed. To HOTR church: when a scared and scarred young girl walked into your service on the 24th November 2013, thank you for welcoming me with opening arms and loving on me since then. You are all dearly cherished in my heart.

Chapter 1

Says The Woman Who Already Has a Man

I'm keeping it 100% real with you guys: being single when you desire to be with someone is hard! Everyone around you seems to be married, getting engaged, or at the very least has met someone new, and yet you can't even remember the last time *Mr. Potential* caught your interest. *"Life sucks,"* you say. Nobody understands what you're going though. You're torn between doing your own thing and finding your own man, or waiting until however long for God to bring you His best. You have days when you're crying out, *"Oh, Lord, when exactly will my time come? Singleness is killing me!"* Only then, to coincidently find yourself in a social setting, lying through your teeth about just how content you are in the single season. How it would take an extraordinary mighty man of God to move you in any kind of way. How you're totally over men and loving being 'free.' In reality though, all it would take would be to hear from a friend of a friend of a neighbour's friend that he attends church, and you're already planning your lives together!

You read a book, come across an Instagram post, hear a testimony or listen to a sermon on the beauty of singleness, and all of a sudden, you're fired up and content with being single. *"This is the time for God to mould me into the woman, the wife, the mother He wants me to be,"* you say. You smile when Genesis 2:18 comes to mind: *"It is not good for the man to be alone. I will make a helper who is just right for him."* Suddenly, you find joy knowing that God hasn't forgotten about His most prized possession: you! But that never lasts long. Before the day is even over, you're back to complaining about just how much of a struggle being single really is! You've fooled yourself into believing that you're just not good enough for marriage – that you do not deserve a husband. That you're destined to remain single like the Apostle Paul (completely disregarding the fact that Paul makes it clear that both being single or married is a gift from God.) Or worse; that you just might have to settle with *Mr. Purposeless* who still lingers around.

Just like that, you've got yourself feeling low. Nobody can tell you anything. Not your best friend who is currently planning her wedding to the guy of her dreams or your pastor's wife who, although you highly admire and respect, couldn't possibly relate to you when her husband stands right by her side as she remarks, *"Your time will come, my dear."*

You're frustrated, irritated, and irked when people tell you to *"enjoy the single season." "Marriage is overrated." "If you're* not happy being alone, then you won't be happy being taken." "If you aren't whole single, you won't be whole married." And you just want to shout from the top of your lungs, *"SAYS THE WOMAN WHO ALREADY HAS A MAN!!!!" Yes, it must be soooooooo difficult, I mean a real NIGHTMARE for you to go home daily to that fine specimen you call your favor. It must be awful to have companionship most people long for and to have legitimate thighs in your bed! I bet you weren't singing that same sweet tune when you were single, and the only thing waiting for you when you got home was a dripping tap!"*

Well, ladies, I am single and have been for 6 years now. (Briefly dating/seeing/experimenting with *Mr. I'm Just Not That Into You* and *Mr. I Will Turn You Into A Christian* during that time doesn't count, does it?) I have no TDH (Tall, Dark, and Handsome) to massage my hand after I finish writing this, and as far as I'm aware, my TDH isn't even on my radar yet, so I understand your frustration. If I can be completely honest, at times, I *still* feel that frustration, but when that fleeting thought of dissatisfaction enters my mind, I don't dwell on it. I don't dwell on not having a man; I dwell on the assignment God has given me to start or complete before I meet my spouse. When I hear of yet another person's engagement, I don't put down or criticise the happy couple; instead, I pray for them and ask God to bless their union. I pray that even the tiniest hint of jealousy in my heart be removed. When I'm feeling lonely, I don't turn to *Mr. Indifferent,* but instead run to the arms of Jesus, because it is He who makes me whole. So what do you do when the feeling of being single seems too much for you to handle?

Scripture tells us that our Christian walk is a marathon, not a sprint (Hebrews 12:1-2.) Yet so many of us see being married as the destination rather than part of the journey. When you realise that the single season is not a pit-stop or a waiting room because you missed your connecting flight to the land of coupledom, only then can you really learn how to appreciate this season and better yet, love it!

In subsequent chapters, I will share with you just how the Lord opened my eyes to enjoy this season in my life. But before we talk about how to overcome our struggle with singleness, I think it's important to explore some of the most common reasons why we struggle with being single in the first place.

Reason 1: Loneliness

The *'perception of reality'* reason!

I don't know about you, but for me, loneliness was the main reason I entertained a lot of guys I had no business entertaining! I ashamedly spent my first few single years giving my number to anyone who asked for it. I didn't care that I wasn't attracted to them, had nothing in common with them, or that they weren't my usual type. I was desperate! I hated not having someone around to talk to. Not having someone to take me out and show me off for the world to see. And more than anything, I hated being alone. But even when I did have *Mr. One Of Many* doing all those things for me, I still felt lonely.

Why? Because I was looking for someone else to fill the void that only Jesus can.

Unconditional love, affection, protection, being needed, feeling desired, having a purpose, and whatever else we feel we lack when we have nobody around – Jesus is waiting and wanting to give us all these things and so much more! Yet, we continue to chase after these things from man instead of from the Source. Is it any wonder then why God hasn't brought you your spouse? He doesn't want you idolising a man you hold responsible for eliminating all your insecurities when only God can do that. (Oh, and FYI; a spouse may mask some insecurities for a while, but he can never remove them. That's why some individuals are unhappy, lonely and insecure WITHIN a Marriage.) Marriage is not the cure for loneliness. If you're in such a hurry to get married or find bae because you hate being alone, you should be thanking God you're still single because you desire something you're not ready for. You're chasing and making yourself available for something you just don't understand. Know that I don't say this to hurt you or be mean. I say it because I understand what it feels like to be lonely. Loneliness is one of the most crushing emotions I have ever felt, and it has made me act out of desperation rather than logic and common sense. I had to realise the hard way that when my mood is based on the reaction and presence of others, I will always feel empty, and you will too.

"But you don't understand my loneliness! I've been single for so long – even longer than you, Miss 6 Years and counting!"

I get it – you probably feel like your situation is different from everyone else's, and therefore you can't relate to their story or even mine. But guess whose story you can relate to? That of King Jesus. The Son of God traded His glorious place on God's right hand side for a life of serving others and experienced the same emotions and pain you're going through. Jesus was lied to (Matthew 26:14, 25.) Lied about (Luke 23:1-2.) Betrayed (Matthew 26:14-16, 69-75.) Insulted and mocked (1 Peter 2:23; John 19:5; Luke 22:63.) Spat on, beaten, and made to carry the heavy cross He would soon be nailed to (John 19:1-3; Matthew 27:26; John 19:17-18.) He experienced loneliness that made Him feel deserted even from God (Mark 15:34), yet in the midst of it all, He knew He was never really alone because God was with Him. Jesus sympathised and experienced human weaknesses and temptation, yet still remained without sin (Hebrews 4:15.) He didn't rush or skip the process He had to go through because He didn't enjoy the feeling associated with it; He endured until the very end because He understood that He needed to go through the process to achieve the desired outcome. Our single season is no different. How can you appreciate the journey of being with someone else when you can't even bear the journey of being by yourself?

Understand that *being* alone and *feeling* lonely are two separate things. Being alone is your actual reality; feeling lonely is your perception of reality – it's based on your state of mind. Right now, I'm alone *(the reality),* but I'm not lonely because I feel God's presence all around me *(my perception).* Therefore, if you're struggling in this area, it's not your circumstances that need changing (i.e., finding bae), but your mind-set. Stop allowing your reality to dictate your state of mind. Yes, your circumstances may show one thing, but it's up to you to believe another. How can you believe that you have the power to move mountains (Matthew 17:20) and walk amongst snakes and scorpions and crush them (Luke 10:19), yet fail to believe you have control over your very own mind?

Beautiful beloved woman of God, as His child know this: You don't ever have to feel lonely because you have the Holy Spirit, God Himself dwelling within you. (1 Corinthians 3:16; John 14:15-17) So continually speak God's promises into your life and immerse yourself in scriptures. When you spend time studying God's word and saturating your life with it, you will build up an instant immunity to loneliness and shut it down the moment it rears its ugly head.

Reason 2: Feeling Purposeless

The *'my life would have purpose if I was a wife'* reason!

Relationship with Christ on point/getting there ☑

Education completed ☑

Great job and/or steady income ☑

Great family and friends ☑

Generally healthy, happy, and content ☑

Bae ☐

I get it – every area in your life seems to be thriving or at the very least doing ok. But what would make your life complete, what would bring you joy you haven't experienced anywhere else seems to be the one thing you just can't acquire. You often find yourself asking, *"What next?"* You're unwilling or unable to move forward because it feels like you're at the stage in your life where the only thing missing is a husband. The last piece of the puzzle you just can't seem to find.

Let me just make this clear to you now – there is absolutely nothing wrong in desiring a spouse. There is absolutely nothing wrong in asking God, *"What next?,"* and there is absolutely nothing wrong with believing the vision God gave you requires both you and your husband to complete. There is something wrong, however, when all you seem to do is eat, sleep, and dream of a husband – so much so that the thought of one becomes your idol. There is something wrong when you feel purposeless because *Mr. But I'm Walking In My Purpose* hasn't shown up yet. And there is definitely something wrong when you begin to disobey God because you know He's told you to do something or go somewhere, but you won't move because you don't have a man by your side to move along with you.

Some of us struggle with singleness because we think a spouse and a family would give us the purpose our lives seem to lack. Yet we fail to understand that if we needed a spouse in the season we were in or a spouse in the season we were going into, we would have one. We fail to understand that the Creator knows what His creation requires. God isn't withholding anything we need. He has said that even birds don't worry about food because He feeds them, so how much more will He take care of you, who is far more valuable than even the rarest and most exotic type of bird? (Luke 12:24.) Even when Adam and Eve sinned against God and were banished from the Garden of Eden, God still made clothing for them before they left (Genesis 3:21). So why do you think God will not equip you with what you need at the very time you need it?

Let's briefly look at the story of Abraham (also known as Abram), who is known as a man of Great Faith in the Bible. God told Abraham to leave his country, relatives, and father's house and go to an unknown land. In exchange for Abraham's obedience, God assured Abraham that he would be greatly rewarded:

"God had told Abram, Leave your own country behind you, and your own people, and go to the land I will guide you to. If you do, I will cause you to become the father of a great nation; I will bless you and make your name famous, and you will be a blessing to many others." (Genesis 12:1-2)

"Abram travelled through the land as far as Shechem. There he set up camp beside the oak of Moreh. At that time, the area was inhabited by Canaanites. Then the Lord appeared to Abram and said, "I will give this land to your descendants." And Abram built an altar there and dedicated it to the Lord, who had appeared to him. (Genesis 12:6-7)

After that, Abram travelled south and set up camp in the hill country, with Bethel to the west and Ai to the east. There he built another altar and dedicated it to the Lord, and he worshiped the Lord. Then Abram continued traveling south by stages toward the Negev. (Genesis 12:8-9)

These passages show that God *told* Abraham the promise – he would give Abraham and his descendants a particular land (Genesis 12:1-2.) God then *showed* him the promise – He showed Abraham the land his offspring would one day own (Genesis 12:6-7.) But as it was not time for the promise to come to pass, Abraham *MOVED* on to another land (Genesis 12:8- 9.) The vision could not come to pass at the time because the land of Canaan was already occupied by the Canaanites. Although the appointed time was approaching, it wasn't yet time for the Canaanites to be evicted from the land. Secondly, the land was promised to Abraham's descendants – Abraham didn't even have a descendant at the time! Even when Abraham settled in another land near Bethel; the promise regarding the land of Canaan still existed, but it just wasn't the right time for it to be obtained.

God has told you the promise (Jeremiah 29:11) and may have even shown you the promise (Joel 2: 28-30) but like Abraham; even when we don't see the promise materialising, let us keep *moving* forward. Delay is not denial. You see weeks, months, and even years of singleness go by and are so frustrated that you fail to see God's work at hand! He's working some things out in the background that if you weren't so occupied feeling 'woe is me,' you just might notice.

"But these things I plan won't happen right away. Slowly, steadily, surely, the time approaches when the vision will be fulfilled. If it seems slow, do not despair, for these things will surely come to pass. Just be patient! They will not be overdue a single day!" - Habakkuk 2:3 (TLB)

Reason 3: All my friends are loved up; don't I deserve to be, too?
The '*self-pity*' reason!

"But all my friends are in relationships..." "But I was single waaay before them so I should be first in line to receive a husband..." "But they only just gave their life to Christ, how come they've met their spouse already....?" "But I've got it all together, so why am I still single....?"

It puzzles you (and probably those around you) that you seem to have everything going but you just can't seem to find/get/keep a man. If your parents are anything like mine, then probably on your graduation day, as soon as you had collected your scroll and walked off the stage like you were the baddest chick in the game, the questions and prophecies started rolling in. *"So the next big thing is marriage?" "Where is your boyfriend?" "By this time next year...."* It got so bad that one day, I had to tell my mum (in the nicest way possible, of course), that my future marriage wasn't about her and what she wanted. It wasn't even about me and what I wanted; it was about God's will and perfect timing over my life.

The thing is, we have all grown up thinking that marriage is the end goal and that if we're not married by a certain age, then something somewhere went wrong. Unfortunately; this misunderstanding is further nurtured by society's standards and other people's unsolicited opinions, to the point that this becomes our desire to rush to the alter. But if you would only block out the noise and let the view of God be your only driving force, then you would realise that marriage isn't God's divine purpose for your life right now; a period of singleness is.

In the book of Genesis, we see that God first made Adam – He didn't make Adam and Eve together – just Adam. In fact, when God first created Adam, there was no plan for Eve at all! God brought to Adam every kind of animal and bird as companion before He brought to Adam someone in His likeness! (Genesis 2:7-23). Adam was instructed to take care of the Garden of Eden (verse 8) and name the diverse range of animals God had formed from the soil (verse 19.) Adam had a purpose that could only be fulfilled in his state of singleness, and it was only *after* Adam began walking in his purpose that God formed Eve because He knew Adam could handle both.

We spend so much time feeling sorry for ourselves and focusing on who we are: *"I'm kind, I look after my home, I'm a prayer worrier, I pay my tithes without fail,"*— that we fail to pay attention to *where we are*. Yes, you can wake up at 3 a.m. to pray and never miss a night vigil, but that doesn't mean you're at a stage in your life where you can deal with the responsibility a partner for life will bring.

If Adam had received Eve at a time when he wasn't ready, do you think he could have nurtured the Garden and Eve at the same time? No, of course not; he would have been distracted because his time would have been split between looking after the Garden and caring for Eve. But because Adam was already managing the Garden before Eve was formed, when she did come along, the foundation had already been set so that he was in a position to give his attention to both.

This is no different from what God requires of us before we meet our spouse; there are just some things that we need to start and/or complete in our state of singleness before our spouse comes along and diverts our attention. However, if the foundation during our single season has already been planted, then even though our attention will be split between our responsibilities, it will not ruin God's purpose for our lives. Even Paul explains that there are just some tasks that require complete concentration that a married person who has to be devoted to his or her first ministry (family) cannot fully commit to:

"I want you to be free from the concerns of this life. An unmarried man can spend his time doing the Lord's work and thinking how to please him but a married man has to think about his earthly responsibilities and how to please his wife. His interests are divided. In the same way, a woman who is no longer married or has never been married can be devoted to the Lord and holy in body and in spirit. But a married woman has to think about her earthly responsibilities and how to please her husband." – (1 Corinthians 7:32–34)

Take this book, for example. I knew it could only be completed during my single season because God made it clear to me that I was to write this book from a Singleton's perspective. During the time of writing, I had guys tell me they believed that I was the one or that they were told I was the one *(by whom is still questionable),* yet with so much confidence, I would tell them they were definitely mistaken because I knew without a doubt in my mind, this book had to be completed before I even entertained my spouse.

I'm telling you, there is this unexplainable peace when you're exactly where God wants you to be, doing exactly what He called you to do.

I can admit that I'm a little too comfortable in this single season however facts are facts: What I have been called to do begins in this season of my life and whatever I go through and learn will equip me for the next season of my life – whatever that may be. I'm not rushing to open a bolted door for which I do not have the keys because that would be silly right? Yet for many of us, we do exactly that when it comes to relationships.

Beautiful beloved woman of God; Trust God, and I mean <u>really</u> trust Him. And if you don't, learn to! Stop saying you trust Him with your lips while your heart is crying out for bae. Stop saying you believe He will bring you a spouse but continue to chase *Mr. Non - Committed.* If you are truly living for God and walking in your purpose, you will be totally unconcerned about still being single. Life doesn't begin the moment you say '*I do.*' Strive to live a life of godliness even if you never utter those words.

Just to give you some perspective, when I was struggling baaaaaaad with singleness *(no typo – I do mean baaaaaaad!),* I had to ask myself this: If the world was to end right now and I had to stand before Jesus, with all that I have achieved so far for His kingdom, would He be proud of me? Would He congratulate me on being effective at using my gifts to share His word, or would He shake His head in disappointment, turn His back on me because I wasted my time waiting for *Mr. But I Fulfilled My Purpose?* It's a serious question you need to ask yourself (and more than once), because if the answer is ever the latter, what exactly is it that you are waiting for?

And if you're not sure what you should be doing in this season, then all you need to do is ask God *(James 1:5-6).* Yes, it really is that simple! The passage actually states that, <u>*"God will give you wisdom and will not rebuke you for asking.*"</u> Stop turning to friends and events for temporary satisfaction and turn to your Creator for your lifelong purpose! You don't need to copy what everyone around you is doing or try a million different things and settle for the easiest of them all. Sit at the feet of Jesus daily and wait for Him to give you direction on what He wants you to do. Sit at His feet no matter how long it takes and He will surely answer you. I did just that, and He instructed me to write this very book!

Reason 4: You want to have sex and not feel guilty (a.k.a. being able to have legitimate sex).
The *'reason we don't want to admit'* reason!

Now I don't know about you, but this definitely applied to me. One of the many reasons I wanted to get married after I got saved was because for me, marriage meant avoiding sexual sin. I knew that sex outside of marriage was wrong *(no matter how you try and argue it, ladies – it is wrong!)* Anyway, I thought, well, if I got married, it would stop this lustful nature inside of me because I would have a spouse who would satisfy all my sexual needs. I got so caught up in the world's standards that tell us that sexual fulfilment is crucial to human happiness that even after I became saved; I carried on thinking this way. (And this is why the renewal of your mind is so important, which I'll talk more about in chapter 3.)

There are so many scriptures that tell us that lust is not of God. (1 John 2:16, Ephesians 5:5, Galatians 5:19-21); therefore, being unable to control your sexual desires and refrain from sexual sin is not a reason to rush to the altar. If you're lusting after someone, even if it's your 'soon to be husband,' that doesn't stop the moment you are pronounced man and wife. You will carry that same lusting spirit into your marriage and eventually lust after someone else.

Don't get me wrong – I'm convinced that God wants married couples to have strong sexual desires for one another. One only has to look in the book of Songs of Songs to understand that God's plan for a healthy marriage includes a strong sexual desire between a husband and wife. But do you really think it makes God happy for the sole purpose of a marriage (or getting into a relationship for the purpose of marriage) to be because two people were lusting after one another and did not trust the Holy Spirit enough to quench their thirst?

When you truly surrender your life to Christ and become one of His very own, you are filled with the Holy Spirit, and through the Holy Spirit, you are given the power to exercise self-control (Galatians 5:22-23.) Therefore, if you find yourself struggling with this very issue, don't indulge your flesh, but walk in the power you already possess!

Reason 5: You think being married will make you a better Christian.
The *'blackmailing God'* reason!

This isn't just about sexual sin, as I've just mentioned – this has to do with struggling with singleness because you believe your spiritual life is the way that it is simply because you are not married. You believe you will stop lusting the moment you get married, stop having your nose in everybody else's business the moment you get married, and stop wanting to go to clubs and getting drunk the moment you get married. Yet you fail to realise that a lusting/worldly/gossiping Singleton only turns into a lusting/worldly/gossiping wife. Marriage won't change that.

I'm going to let you in on 3 regular conversations I used to have with my bestie J (Jesus) at the beginning of my single season to further explain this point:

Conversation 1:

J: *"Should you really be wearing such a low cut top?"*

Me: *"Well, I wouldn't if I was married because I would only then be trying to please my husband, but I'm not, soooo..."*

Conversation 2:

J: *"Why do you entertain that guy you have no interest in?*

Me: *"Because I'm single, so I can. When I get married, obviously I won't act like this."*

Conversation 3:

J: *"Does it matter that you didn't use that plate? Wash it up anyway."*

Me: *"Nope, no way, I'm nobody's slave! I clean up after myself. Why can't others do the same?"*

J: *"So when you get married, is that what you're going to tell your husband?"*

Me: *"It's going to be different with my husband because that will be my role as a wife, but that time hasn't come yet, so I'm not washing that plate!"*

Don't these conversations sound pathetic? But the truth is, we justify not being great women of God because we tell ourselves that unless we live a certain lifestyle, make a certain amount of money, or have a great man by our side then being obedient is a requirement we just can't fulfil. We believe that the lack of our desires coming to pass is hindering us from living a godly lifestyle. What we fail to understand however is that God requires us to live holy in spite of our desires! *"Like, Lord, I want to obey you – I really do. But I need to get a few things in order first!" "I'll truly surrender to You when you turn current bae into a Christian." "I'll stop talking to so many guys when I meet the one." "I'll stop living like a slob when I'm living with my husband." "I'll start being respectful to my elders when I meet my man's family."* Yeah, right!

The thing is, being obedient doesn't always make sense and it certainly isn't easy! Sometimes the Lord will ask me to do something, and I'm like, *"J, it really ain't that deep!"* But God knows exactly what He's doing and why He's asking, so who am I to question that? Obedience only requires understanding the *'how'* to do something, and not the *'why.'*

When God used to ask me to wash up a plate left in the sink (*that I didn't use btw – just putting that out there!*), I was adamant that I wasn't going to do it! I used to fight with God about washing up just one plate. I would be at work, and God would still be reminding me to wash it when I got home. At the time, I used to say to God, *"I know what you're trying to do and the point you're trying to make. You want me to get into the habit of washing plates now so that I will do it with ease when I get married. But the thing is, I will have no problem doing all of this but only when I'm married."*

It's only as my faith in Christ started to grow that I realised the true meaning of washing that plate. Yes, it helped to train me for the future, but the actual reason was because God wanted to see if I would be obedient to His voice, starting with the little things. Starting with the things that seemed so trivial to me yet had deeper meaning beyond the obvious. When I still wouldn't obey (*yes, I can be a disobedient child*), God used to say to me, *"How do you expect me to trust you with a family when you can't even take care of a home?" "How do you expect your husband to listen to you when you won't even listen to me?"* The plate itself wasn't the issue, but God was showing me that He can't trust me with a lot when He can't even trust me with a little *(Luke 19:11-26)*.

You need to stop kidding yourself and thinking that a husband will make you a better Christian and more obedient to God. If God's consistent and unconditional love can't change you; if His mercies and blessings or the sacrifice He's made don't move you, what makes you think a husband – who will at times annoy you, get on your last nerve, and maybe even cause you to question whether you should have married him in the first place – change you? You expect God to bring you His best, His most prized possession, the apple of His eye and give him to you to hold onto, to love, and to nurture; yet He can't even trust you with less valuable things. Marriage won't change you, but you do need to change before marriage. So stop running from this guy to that guy, this self-help book to that self-help book, this new wave of thinking to that new wave of thinking, and run to the only permanent solution: God.

Reason 6: The clock is ticking
The *"If not now, when?"* reason!

I was 23 when I started dating *Mr. I'm Just Not That In To You*. He was a great guy. Very good looking, had his own home, a great job, and a nice car *(or so I thought, but that's a story for another day!)* However, we had absolutely no chemistry and he definitely didn't 'wow' me. In hindsight, he didn't seem that in to me either yet in spite of all this, I continued to force myself to have feelings for him *(it was hard!)* And we dated for about 6 months. '*Why was I with someone I didn't like*' you ask? Simple; because I had given myself a timetable to be married by 25, and he just happened to be the not-so-lucky guy around at the time. He seemed too good to be true *(I realised later he was!)* and even though I didn't have any genuine feelings for him, I was prepared to force myself to love him because I was desperate to get married by *my* time. I broke off whatever it was we had going on the day I gave my life to Christ, but who knows? I could have ended up with someone who wasn't right for me just because he fitted in with my plans at the time.

Let's keep it real. Some of us are willing to settle down with guys we know we're not meant to be with because we allow our own plans and desires to rule our lives. We genuinely want to surrender our life to Christ. We move away from toxic friends, break old habits, devote time to God, yet all the while, we are subconsciously praying that God's will aligns with ours. We are praying that God's timetable correlates with our own, and then we get depressed when we turn one year older and there's still no hubby in sight.

"Slowly, steadily, surely, the time approaches when the vision will be fulfilled. If it seems slow, wait patiently, for it will surely take place. It will not be delayed." - Habakkuk 2:3

"There is a time for everything, a season for every activity under heaven." - Ecclesiastes 3:1

God is clear when He says, "Seek first the Kingdom of God" (Matthew 6:33). He doesn't want us concerned about earthly things over which He has full dominion and could give us in a heartbeat if that was what we needed. He wants us to be focused on our spiritual lives, which He chooses not to control. He wants us to love and serve Him because we want to; not because we have to (free will.) How can you believe God parted the Red Sea, woke Lazarus from the dead, delivered the Israelites out of Egypt, and caused an old barren woman named Hannah to have a child, yet doubt the same God will move in your present situation? Our God is not a respecter of persons (Romans 2:11). If He can do it for them, He will certainly do it for you!

Don't compromise your faith and His promise over your life based on manmade time. If you're not married at 30, it's not because you didn't attend every event you were invited to, didn't talk to every guy who showed interest, or because you followed your intuition and cut off *Mr. Good For Nothing*. It's because it's not your time, and you need to trust that everything happens at an appointed time. (Ecclesiastes 3:1-15.)

Now 26, and sitting in a coffee shop with a cup of Green Tea that I don't even like, (but have to buy something to sit in and can't afford anything else!) I'm looking back over my life, and

I'm thankful that I didn't get married any earlier. I was a complete mess from the age of 10 until 24. A few days after my 24th birthday, I gave my life to Christ but still loathed men. Then, I went from one extreme of hating men to desperately wanting to marry one (anyone!), which consumed me and became my idol. This simmered down just before I turned 25. Ever since then, I've been too concerned with seeking God's face and getting to know Him more to look up and notice anyone else. I could have potentially ruined a guy's life and delayed both our purposes because I wanted something for which I was not ready for. Don't rush to do the same. Chill.

Reason 7: Singleness makes us feel undesirable.
The *"what's wrong with me"* reason!

To some, singleness makes us feel undesirable to the opposite sex, and to others, singleness confirms the thoughts in our minds that tell us we don't 'deserve' a man. The older we get and the longer we've spent being single, the more we believe this to be true.

Beautiful beloved woman of God; I can't make this any clearer, but I need you to understand that when God created you, He created a masterpiece (Ephesians 2:10). Society says your nose is too big or flat, your hips are too wide or not wide enough, your eyes are too far apart or too close together, your hair is too kinky or too fine, your skin is too dark or not dark enough, your lips are too big or too thin, and whatever else. But when the Creator looks at you, He sees perfection. He sees flawlessness. Nothing is out of proportion, and you are exactly right because you were created in His image, and God doesn't create junk nor make mistakes (Genesis 1:27).

Therefore, since you have been perfectly made, how you feel is based on your lack of confidence and your misunderstanding of what desire is. You lack confidence because you don't believe your inner and outer attributes to be enough, and you misunderstand what desire is because you believe it has to be shown to you by man even though it has, it is and will always be shown to you by God.

Confidence:

"The quality of being certain of your abilities or of having trust in people, plans, or the future."

The truth is, you can buy all the MAC make-up in the world, wear the longest and finest weaves, have an amazing figure and rock the most expensive name brands, and still feel like you resemble Gollum *(you know who that is right?)* Confidence and beauty have nothing to do with what you look like and everything to do with what you feel like on the inside of you. Even on my worst days, I still feel beautiful. Even when I've gone to the shops and left my eyebrows at home, I feel beautiful. Even when it's a struggle to get my hair into a hairband, I feel beautiful, and even when people tell me I'm too slim, I look too young, and there's not much going on in the rear end, I still recognize the masterpiece that I am.

Did I always feel this way? Absolutely not. But I came to realise that my physical appearance is just a mask that fades away with age (Proverbs 31:30), and it's my inner attributes that actually make me beautiful.

Your kindness, devotion to Christ, smile, sense of humour, facial expressions, the change in your voice when you're happy, being approachable, being different, doing things outside the box, being sociable and making everyone feel special – these are the things that make you beautiful. Although they are not all physical attributes, they all radiate outward and enhance your overall beauty. I'm not saying there is anything wrong with makeup and looking good, but it shouldn't be for the acceptance of everyone else. Yes, the world focuses on what you look like on the outside, but the One who actually matters cares about what you look like on the inside (1 Samuel 16:7). So great – your eyebrows are naturally arched, but can you pray for others?

Desire:

"A strong feeling of wanting to have something or wishing for something to happen"

Sis, God desires you!

> ➢ He desires that you be saved and come to the knowledge of the truth (1 Timothy 2:4).
> ➢ He desires that you know Him personally (Acts 17:27).
> ➢ He desires to have a friendship with you (James 2:23).
> ➢ He desires that you trust Him completely (Jeremiah 29:11).

> He desires that as His child and His friend, you not be ashamed or scared to ask anything from Him (James 1:5).

> He desires that you don't run away in shame when you stumble, but go to Him and confess your sins so He can make you righteous (1 John 1:9).

> He desires that you know just how much He desires and loves you! (John 3:16).

I get it; it seems like nobody's paying you any attention right now, but God is always paying you attention, and He wants you to know that He is more than enough. No man can ever measure up to the Lord; therefore, whatever it is your lacking won't change even when a guy does come into the picture. God knows what you desire and has promised to grant you the desires of your heart (Psalm 37:4), so how about you take delight in Him first? It must break our Father's heart that we desire mere men more than we desire Him.

DISCLAIMER! If you're looking for a book to comfort you until *Mr. Potential* comes into your life; you might have already realised, this isn't it! Although I sympathise and can defiantly relate; my assignment isn't to console you in this season. My assignment is to make it clear, you are to find contentment in whatever season you are in (Philippians 4:12). So that means there is joy to be experienced even as a Singleton!

I've definitely had my own struggles with singleness so I understand what you're going through, but it hurts my heart to see women go through what I've been through and make terrible choices simply because they hate being alone.

After I had wasted so much time on random dudes, I went through a period in my life where past experiences damaged me so much that I didn't even want to get married (it didn't help that I also despised men at this point). I thought I had it all figured out: I was going to become a Financial Crime Investigator, write a fiction book that would be turned into a movie and hit the big screen and make me mega rich, and when I was around 30 years old, I would carry myself to a sperm bank and have a child or two that way *(It might sound ridiculous now, but at the time, this was my perfect future!)*.

A few months after I got saved, I started having this strong desire for a husband. - *Yes Christina – Member of the 'You Fine All By Yourself' Association; Leader of 'He Who Finds, Not She Who Looks' Movement; Secretary of the 'I'm So Buried In Christ I Can't See Anyone Else Council'* was thirsty for a man (I know!) But It completely blew my mind. I was newly saved and so consumed with the desire for a husband that it became my idol. I became obsessed with the idea of marriage and a man but both never came, and so as the months went by, I started to get angry with God. I would remind Him that He created the desire in my heart for a spouse, so where exactly was my knight in shining armour? I would get on my knees, begging Him that if He wasn't going to give me a spouse right away, then could He please just take away this unexplainable craving I had for one. I pleaded with Him that it wasn't fair for me to desire something I was never going to have.

One day, I got so frustrated with the desire for a spouse that I actually accused God of taunting me with a spouse He knew He was never going to give me. I was so angry I began to cry and told myself that I was done being a Christian because it was just too hard. I was just about to reach out to *Mr. But Why Haven't I Cut You Off Yet?*, when in that moment, God reminded me just how much He loved me. He showed me I had spent years finding my worth in the eyes of guys, and He wasn't going to allow me to become dependent on another human being ever again. He told me it would take time to mould me into His image – that I was a mess and broken, but He would heal me. He told me that the desire He had given me was to remind me of His promise concerning my life, and that at the right, appointed time, it would happen.

So you see, I haven't always felt comfortable with being single. It took some time to get to this stage, but I just got so fed up with doing it my way and failing miserably that I decided to give God's way a chance. He restored in me everything that was lacking and that I thought I would find in a spouse. When I reflect on just how far God's taken me, I'm at a loss for words because I never thought it possible to ever be at peace about my situation and myself. I'm even at the point where I'm completely happy and content in this season, and one thing I wholeheartedly do not desire right now is a man!

I know some of us have reached that stage of wanting to give up – where our tears of longing have become tears of frustration. Some of us cry ourselves to sleep at night because we are yearning for something that hasn't come to pass. Some of us are depressed for days when we hear the news that another one of our friends is getting married, and some of us have been burned so deeply in the past that we're done with guys altogether. I too have suffered from all of those stages, even after I gave my life to Christ. I was single then, and I'm still single now, but my mind-set has changed. I don't look like what I've been through, but understand I didn't jump out of my mother's womb on fire for Christ. I've been battered by the world and pruned by God, and it's been difficult. I've dealt with my own set of heartbreaks, setbacks, abuse, injustices, and loneliness. I've gone through things I wouldn't even wish on my worst enemy if I had one, but I've learned *(and I'm still learning)* to trust in God and to not let my present circumstances dictate the rest of my life.

So if you've been doing it your way for so long now, ever since you can remember, and it's still not gotten you very far, are you open to trying it God's way? Or will you keep doing the same thing time and time again and expecting different results? *(They call that insanity btw – just putting it out there!)* No matter how bad your life currently looks, how bad you've lived in the past or even as a Christian, the mistakes you've made, there is absolutely nothing too difficult for God to change and make anew. So with that being said, the next chapter was written specifically to encourage you that no matter the struggle, sin or whatever it is you've had to sacrifice for temporary satisfaction; God is more than able to turn your situation around. The question is: Will you let Him?

Chapter 2

A Singleton's Struggle With Singleness

My Story:

Growing up, I had a relatively happy childhood and was blessed with amazing family! I have always felt extremely lucky to have my mum, who has this never-ending strength and resilience for life that I highly admire; my foster mum, who sadly passed away but loved me as if I was her own; and my foster dad, who is the best father on earth I could ever ask for. The love both my parents have for their children is unexplainable.

As you can imagine, having 2 sets of parents who were so different from each other was incredible and exciting, and my childhood was anything but boring! Even so, people never overlooked a black child to white parents in the early 90s and in a small, isolated town in Cambridgeshire, England. At the time, my sister and I seemed to be the first black people the people in the village had ever seen, and so the long stares and looks of confusion on people's faces when they saw us walking hand-in-hand with our parents and the whispering that usually accompanied it didn't go unnoticed. I hated and felt guilty about the unwanted attention the family seemed to receive while being out with us and always felt ashamed that my foster parents were getting all this unwarranted attention and mistreatment because of the colour of our skin. Although my foster parents went above and beyond to never make us feel different, I was aware that we stood out like sore thumbs, which was only further amplified by school kids in the playground.

I became very self-conscious at an early age and hated everything about myself. We were different to everyone else around, but I thought different meant ugly. Our skin colour was different, our names were weird compared to everyone else's names that were simple and easy to pronounce, and our hair wasn't long and didn't fall weightless behind our backs and around our ears like others seemed to; it was short, thick, and the hairstyles that our peers wore were difficult if not impossible to achieve with our hair texture.

Although I loved my foster parents dearly, I grew up never knowing why we were living with them and not my biological mum. So not only did I feel excluded in the community; I felt rejected and abandoned as well.

A few years later, my sister and I were living back in London with my biological mum, attending a new school, and making new friends. My mother, a single mother at the time, had to support her family here as well as back home in Nigeria meant she was always working and not around often. As I suffered from abandonment issues, I became quickly attached to anyone who did show me any kind of attention which followed me into adulthood. When my obsessive behaviour got too much for whoever was my idol at the time and they distanced themselves from me, I would go through the pain of rejection all over again.

When I was 10 years old, a family friend who I referred to as 'uncle' started showing interest in me. It started with an inappropriate comment here and there and a 'harmless' touch one too many times. Eventually, his subtle grooming turned into sexual abuse, which stopped after I plucked up the courage to tell my mum. That was it: I didn't see him again until a few years later. That period in my life however became the starting point of my downward spiral and exposed me to things that I wasn't ready for at such a young age.

Fast forward a few years, and I literally happened to be at the wrong place at the wrong time when I was physically assaulted and raped by a complete stranger. I was beaten repeatedly until I finally caved in and gave him exactly what he was after. Too humiliated and scared to go to the police or tell my family, I instead confided in who I thought were close friends at the time. But before I knew it, what seemed like everyone in my secondary school had heard about what had happened, but not as it had happened; instead, the part about me being assaulted and forced against my will was left out. In its place, I was portrayed as having fully consented to what had happened and was bullied as a result of being seen as sexually loose. I felt crushed. All kind of rumours about me spread fast and the victim in all this was quickly seen as the perpetrator.

Mentally I pretended not to care and forced myself to forget about past events, but physically, I was self-harming to cope with everything. To everyone else, I seemed like a normal teenager who always had a smile firmly plastered across her face, but behind closed doors, I was a complete mess. I felt neglected by everyone, unworthy, unloved, and I hated myself. I just couldn't cope, and the façade of this happy-go-lucky girl was becoming more and more difficult to maintain.

This continued for a few more years until I had my first serious boyfriend. He wasn't from the same area as me so he knew nothing of this girl I was portrayed as. So with him, I felt for the very first time that I could be myself. But as myself, I was fragile, insecure, possessive, and dependent. I felt neglected by everyone else, so I had this constant need to feel loved at all times by him. I was an absolute headache to that poor guy and gave him hell! A good day at work or university for him was a bad day when he got back home! I thought I should have been the only person making him happy, so if I wasn't, there was a problem. I had no sense of identity beyond being his girlfriend and often questioned why he 'loved' me when I couldn't even love myself. I put up with a lot of crap in the relationship and others after that simply because I was so desperate to keep a guy – *any* guy!

We were together for a few years, but during that time, he would randomly cut off all contact with me and used to break up with me regularly. I think he liked the control he could clearly see he had over me, and we both knew I wasn't going anywhere, so I put up with it and often found myself begging him to stay with me! I saw myself as damaged goods, a rotten apple. Even though I was extremely unhappy in the relationship, I reasoned that I should be counting my lucky stars that at least someone wanted me. Whenever we had broken up, out of the blue he would randomly invite me to his house, making it clear what he wanted. He would woe me into his bed only to chuck me out right after the deed was done. Even though I felt cheap and used, I would make myself available every time because I thought if I just gave him what he wanted, he would give me what I wanted, which was security and the title of belonging to someone. When that never happened, I would become emotionally abusive towards him *(to call my mouth sharp is an understatement – poor guy!)*. He broke up with me for the last time, and once more, my world crumbled.

I had the title of his girlfriend for years, which I found comfort in, and before that, I was known as all sorts of derogatory names. I felt like I was going back to the negative names I was called because I couldn't see myself beyond what other people saw me as. I lost my identity as his girlfriend and hated the person left behind. I had given myself in every way that I could to this guy, and he had happily taken it but walked away when he got bored, leaving me more broken than when he found me. My security net was ripped from under me, and I just couldn't cope with being me.

I became depressed, suffered from panic attacks, stopped eating, overdosed on sleeping tablets, and drank alcohol throughout the day just so that I wouldn't have to cope with reality. I was so good at pretending that nobody suspected anything, yet at the same time hated that nobody could see that my cry for help was actually a cry for help. The pain I had masked for the past few years and the pain I was currently going through reached a climax, and it was only a matter of time before I exploded.

Although I thought I had hit rock bottom before, one particular evening I felt like the rubble underneath rock bottom. There had been many times before that I had dreamed of taking my life. As the years went by, this manifested into trying to take my life, but the fear of hell and ending up there petrified me, so I would inflict just enough pain on myself to suffer, but not enough to end it all. Yet this day, I had reached a point where even hell didn't scare me. I had decided that I had nothing to lose by being here; nobody would even notice that I was gone. As I sat against the wall on my bedroom floor, I swallowed every pill I could find in my house and waited for the consequences. I wanted to die that day and surely took enough pills that I should have. So I was inconsolable when I woke up the very next day with the worst headache I've ever had. You would have thought I would be thanking God, right? But no – I did the complete opposite: I was so angry with Him!

I thought He saved me to watch me suffer; I hated who I thought God was. Why couldn't He just let me have the peace I desired by letting me end it all? Couldn't He see that I didn't want to be here – that I was done with my life and no longer wanted to carry on? Yet even in my state of anger, I couldn't deny that God had saved me from taking my own life for a purpose. I couldn't understand it then, but I knew I should have been dead. Yet there I was, broken but still alive.

I wish I could say after that miraculous night that I submitted my life to Christ, but I didn't. You see, God forces nothing on us – not salvation, not peace, not joy, not a spouse, not even faith; these things are a choice we all must make. To surrender your life means to give it up by choice. He won't take it by force. So I made the choice to keep blaming God for all the pain other people had inflicted on me and continue living in sin. I made the choice to get my heart hurt over and over again and to find my self-worth in Mr. *Flavour Of The Month*.

I suffered from loneliness and only felt desired when I had a guy showing interest in me, so I would make myself available at all costs for some sort of attention and validation. When I finally bagged a dude, the relationships were always short-lived, as the relationships survived on attraction only. Although on the outside I looked desperate for any sort of relationship, on the inside, I was a closed book, showed no emotion, and even physical touch of any sort was extremely uncomfortable for me. My actions said it all: *"Compliment me and feed my self-esteem all day long, but don't you dare touch me!"* My mood was always based on the state of a relationship and whether I was in one or not. If a guy was showing interest in me, I was the happiest girl alive, but if there was nobody giving me attention, I became depressed and suicidal. I was put on anti-depressants, but it wasn't long before I started abusing them too, and it became this never ending cycle in which I would go from one guy to the next (most of the time back to the same guys), only to find myself in the same situation. When everything seemed great, so was I, but then as soon as we had broken up, I broke down with the relationship.

I was dating *Mr. I'm Just Not That In To You* when I realised that I could no longer continue in this never-ending cycle; I was physically and mentally drained, and I literally had nothing left to give to anyone else. Yet God was ok with that. He wanted me even in my broken state and loved me just as I came. Even though I was finally making a choice to love Him, He had chosen to love me from the very beginning. So on the 24th November, 2013, I surrendered my life to Christ, and here I am today. ☺

Even though I've only been a Christian for 3 years, for as long as I can remember, I have always known about God. I attended church every Sunday when I moved back to London with my mum, but I never had a relationship with God. I prayed when I wanted something and read my Bible sporadically. I was more concerned about striving to live a morally good life and being a nice person than anything else. I knew sin was separating me from God but told myself that as soon as I was older and settled, when I got married, or just before I died, I would give my life to Christ *(the 'blackmailing God' reason)* simply because I didn't want to go to hell, and I thought it would be easier to do it then. I was a very religious person. It didn't matter how tired, how drunk, or whatever I had just gotten up to a few minutes earlier, there wasn't a night that went by in which I didn't say Grace just in case I didn't see the next morning.

I constantly felt guilty over the double life I was living because I knew better but didn't do better. I would sleep over at my boyfriend's house but then wake up early in the morning to read my Bible and attend church service. I would constantly look down on people who lived exactly the same lifestyle as me but just didn't enter a building every Sunday morning and thought I was better than them even though I was the hypocrite. I remember one day sitting in church and listening to the sermon while texting *Mr. Flavour of the Month* to see what time we were hooking up after service and what bar we were going to. It was such a struggle living on the fence that I decided I was going to jump right off it. I made a choice and ashamedly choose the temporary gratifications of the world. I stopped attending church and removed myself from anything to do with God, which gave the enemy full control to run riot in my life.

Fast forward November 2013, I'm about 6 months into dating *Mr. I'm Just Not That In To You*. You know how some guys do anything to woo you and promise you the moon and the stars? But as soon as they win you over, they coincidently do not have the time for you? Anyway, I could see the pattern forming – I was watching myself falling apart over feeling rejected by yet another person, and I just thought to myself, *"I can't do this again;" "I can't keep feeling like this;" "When does it end?"* Yet I was too insecure to end the relationship, so I stayed put but became even more distant than normal.

Since I wasn't attending church, a close friend of mine always invited me to hers. Yet every time she did, something 'came up.' I would even lie and tell her that I was regularly attending another church so she wouldn't keep bugging me come to hers. Anyway, this particular Sunday, I decided to attend her church and put a stop to what I perceived as her constant nagging (shout out Theresa!)

I had such a heavy heart this particular Sunday when I walked into House on The Rock London. I didn't even want to be there; I just wanted my friend to stop inviting me. Yet as the pastor started preaching, I was moved to tears just by being in God's presence. I sat there crying with tears rolling down my face, too stunned to wipe them away. God had always been close, but for the first time in my entire life, I felt Him. I gave my life to Christ that very morning and ended it with *Mr. I'm Just Not That In Too You.*

This relationship with Christ was totally different from all the others I had ever had in the past. For the first time in my entire life, I knew that this relationship would never leave me broken; it would never leave me rejected, empty, or depressed. It wasn't a relationship of convenience; I didn't give and give and receive nothing back. I never felt disgusted with myself, cheap, or used, and I never felt that I had to prove myself. I came to God wrecked, lost, and angry, and He accepted me just as I was. I didn't have to pretend to be someone I wasn't or someone He wanted me to be because He knew who I was behind the façade I was so good at putting up, and He loved me regardless.

Even when I didn't love myself, He loved me. Even when I felt rejected by everyone else, He wanted me – flaws and all. He gave me hope – unconditional, unquestionable, and undoubtable love. I felt like it was just He and I against the world. I felt protected, cherished, and precious. He was my protector that I had spent years searching for – He was my Saviour! I had spent years chasing one guy to the next in the hope of being loved, but here the Lord was, His arms wide open, telling me He had loved me from the very beginning. His love wasn't based on what I done for him; His love was based on what He had done for me on the cross. All the titles I had accepted from everyone else were stripped away and instead were replaced with the title of "His child," "His joy," and the "apple of His eye."

As I got to know the Lord, I realised just how much of a wreck I was. Still, He never gave up on me. He first began healing me, teaching me that I could no longer carry un-forgiveness and resentment in my heart. Although I had not received apologies from those who had hurt me, I still had to forgive them and move on. He brought me out of being in bondage from people, and I learnt to rely solely on Him. He gave me fulfilment and a life I actually wanted to live. I had no idea at the time that I would be writing this book, yet I still felt like my life had purpose, which I was determined to walk in one day. He began moulding me in His image and taught me to love what He loves and hate what He hates. For once I wasn't interested in a man's attention; I just wanted the Lord's, and I always had it. He was loving but firm towards me and wouldn't allow me to throw myself a pity party every time I was reminded of the past; instead, He reminded me that comfort, peace, and purpose were all found in Him.

If you knew the broken, insecure, people-dependent, angry girl I used to be, and you saw the beautiful, God-fearing, God-dependent, confident woman I have become, you wouldn't believe it. I am a testimony of how God can completely change someone's life. No matter how bad it looks, there is no situation He cannot change.

Tears roll down my eyes when I'm reminded of such a dark period in my life, and that's why, for the rest of my days, even if I never get married, even if it seems like everything I have ever wanted I never receive, I will serve and honour the Lord with my whole heart – because He is it for me. I know what He delivered me from, and the same God who did it for me can and will (if you let him) do it for you. So, to all my sisters who are in ungodly and/or unhappy relationships, to those who are struggling with being single, to those who are single mothers and believe no guy will be interested in you because you don't come to the relationship alone, to those who are insecure and have settled, and for those who are dependent on someone else for love, attention, and validation: I pray that as you read this, the love the Lord has for you overwhelms you and you have a personal encounter with Him. I pray that at the mention of His name, you experience unexplainable peace that consumes you and your situation in Jesus' mighty Name. Amen.

I felt it important to share my story because as uncomfortable as it is to be so brutally open; I want you to see for yourself that no matter your past, God loves you, He wants you and designed you for a specific purpose no matter what your situation currently looks like. A man's love is temporary, and you do yourself such an injustice to continue to search for it, break your back for it and lower your standards for it when God desires you exactly as you are; flaws and all but only if you allow Him into your life.

Beloved woman of God: When it comes to Him, don't be afraid to speak out! Cry out! Scream out! Do whatever you need to do, but do not continue to suffer in silence. He already knows what you've been through and continues to go through and how much you need a Saviour, but He wants you to usher Him into your life. He won't push, bang, or tackle His way in. Even if you don't know what to say, just start with telling Him that you need Him, that you're a hot mess, that you are desperate for a change, and that you surrender your life to Him. I promise you, He will lead you from there.

Don't give up, sis! I know you're struggling and feel like nobody understands what you're going through and nobody has had it as bad as you have it, but God understands. God knows about your past. He knows how many tears fall from your precious face at night, and He knows how much you long to be wanted by someone that it physically hurts. But only He can heal the pain. All He asks for you in return is that you trust Him, cling to Him, and never let go.

Believe me when I say this: You will never be truly happy no matter what a guy promises you or no matter how long he sticks around because you will always end up compromising yourself to keep him, and you will always fail because he was never designed to be your everything, and you were never designed to be his. You were designed to be your husband's help meet, and your wholeness can only come from God; not from any other human being *(Isaiah 2:22)*. Once you realise that and you let God's amazing love consume you, you will realise that everything else – even when you thought you were deeply, truly, head-over-heels in love – was inadequate to what you truly deserved. God's love for you will always be more than you will ever need, and it's eternal. How amazing is that!

So if you're all cried out, ready for a change, want to forgive and move on, but don't know how to; if you're tired of living the cycle you're currently in, if you want a life that has purpose and meaning or want to find your self-worth in someone other than *Mr. What Are You Thinking*? Then turn over to the next chapter for answers to these issues and more.

Chapter 3

So What's Next?

From Struggle To Contentment

Ok, so you're ready! Ready for change. Ready to fully surrender your life to Christ. Ready to move from a struggling Singleton to a satisfied one. Ready to amend *Mr. Self-Indulgence to Mr. Pain & Misery* in your phone book *(or delete him altogether)* and finally ready to get out of that never-ending cycle you find yourself in. Yet, after the 'buzz' or that 'warm fuzzy feeling' wears off, you may find yourself asking, "*What next?*" Like, how do you go from *"curse the day I met you"* to *"God bless you, my brother,"* when you randomly bump into that ex who cheated on you? How do you go from envying the newest engaged couple to praying for them when you hear of their good news? How do you find joy in the current season you're in when you still feel the same hurt, pain and shame you did before you made the decision to trust God? How do you get to the point where you embrace this season and find yourself truly content in it? Even able to encourage those still struggling with the very things you used to?

As I already explained in the last chapter, God will truly guide you through the process, and no matter how you might feel, you are never left to just figure it out on your own (Isaiah 41:10). However, from personal experience and having witnessed God transform the lives of others going through similar situations, I've learned that there are particular areas in life we need to deal with to reach a point where we are fulfilled and content in the season we are in. Right now, we are in the Wilderness, and there are certain Giants we will need to slaughter, land we will need to cover, and rules we will need to follow before reaching the land of Milk and Honey. But like the Israelites, no matter how long it takes, we will arrive at our destination with God having gone before us every step of the way.

So how does one truly go from struggle to contentment?

1) Come As You Are:
Though your sins are like scarlet, I will make them as white as snow. Though they are red like crimson, I will make them as white as wool. – Isaiah 1:18

So there's this gospel track that I've kinda, sorta, head over heels fallen in love with. It's by an amazing gospel artist, Donnie McClurkin, and the lyrics couldn't be truer:

Come as you are, bring every burden
Come as you are, bring all your shame
Come as you are, I know you hurting
But when you call upon His name
And surrender, surrender
You never be the same.
Come as you are, all who are broken
Come as you are, and find His grace
Come as you are, His arms are open
Let go and let God just have His way
And surrender, surrender
And you never be the same
Come as you are, your pace is over
Come as you are, bring every chain
Come as you are, He holds your future
All things are new, this is the day
To surrender, surrender
Never be the same

Just like the lyrics say, God wants you to come to him just as you are. That means He doesn't care *how* you come to Him, just as long as you come. So what you're not perfect? You're hurting, broken, burdened, defeated, empty, insecure, feel unworthy, or have done a bunch of unimaginable things in your past? He doesn't care about any of that! The truth is, Jesus came to save people just like you! He said Himself that He hasn't come to help those who already think they're good enough; He's come to help sinners turn away from their sin, to help the sick get better (Luke 5:31-32.) Other people disqualify you for the very thing that God qualifies you for. He delights when you choose Him. Angels rejoice when even one person turns away from evil and turns to God (Luke 15:10).

So what are you waiting for? What continues to sabotage you from knowing your Father on a personal level and allowing Him to heal you? Why are you years later, still just a churchgoer, hand lifter, offering giver, but not a genuine Friend of God? What is holding you back from truly surrendering your life to Christ? In the midst of your tears and struggles, why is God still not an option?

Very few people deny the existence of God, so why is it that we still don't know Him on a personal level? The problem is, for those that don't know God; you have this distorted image of Him. You view Him as either this wondering spirit or a Caucasian male with long grey hair, older than time itself, sitting on a throne beyond the skies and looking down on all of us while judging each and every one of our sins and waiting for the next time we mess up. Because you have this view of Him, you feel like you have to strive to be perfect in His sight. Perfection is a hard bar to measure up to and one you know you will never achieve. Perfection causes you to run away from Him instead of embrace Him.

Do you know what's so amazing about God? He created you and adores what He created. He loves you regardless of your past mistakes. Before you were even shaped in your mother's womb, He knew all about you. Before you saw the light of day, He had great plans for you. Before you were even able to sin, He made provisions on the cross for you, and before you even had a debt to pay, your debts were paid (Jeremiah 1:5). You do yourself such an injustice in believing anything else but that; in thinking that you have to come to God perfect when perfection isn't a requirement.

If God only wanted us when we were blemish free, a lot of people wouldn't be who they are and where they are today. If God only required perfection, I for one wouldn't be writing this book because I am far from perfect. If the bar God set was faultlessness, I would never have experienced the joy of the Lord and His immeasurable love. I would still be rotting away in sin, or more accurately, dead right now. So ladies, I beg of you; never feel like you're not good enough to come to God because no matter what you do, and in spite of all you do, nothing can separate you from the love of God (Romans 8:31-32).

HOWEVER *(yes there is a 'however in all of this!)* Having the knowledge that God loves you unconditionally and that the penalty for your sins have already been forgiven does not give you a licence to stay sinning.

I remember the first time I hurt my arm *(I've broken it 3 times, sprained it once, and had pencil lead stabbed into my arm and bloodstream – all from playing rough!)* The first time I had an incident with my arm, my mum practically cried as I cried and was beyond sympathetic. She cradled me in her arms as she reminded me that I wasn't a boy *(although I very much acted like one)* and that I couldn't play rough. Incident 2, and she's still sympathetic but her tone is more irritable this time. She reminds me yet again that I can't play like the boys I chase around the playground play. Incident 3, and she's had gone from, *"Don't play rough,"* to, *"Don't play at all"* during her scolding. Incident 4; I decided to chill with an unattended broken arm for a whole day because I knew if I told her I had hurt my arm once again, I would have had a few more broken bones by the time she had finished with me.

See, the first time I hurt my arm, I didn't know any better. My mum understood my immaturity so she wasn't angry, but she warned me to be careful. Incident 2, and my mum was sympathetic while convinced I was hard of hearing. Incident 3, her sympathy had waned, and I was disciplined for my disobedience. By this time, I knew better than to play rough, but the fun of it far outweighed the consequences. By Incident 4 and 5, I was a lost cause. She no longer told me not to play rough or not to play at all. Instead, she waited for me to seriously hurt myself because she realised I needed to find out the hard way that I could not afford to be so careless with my body *(numerous incidents after this including being run over, I finally reached this conclusion!)*

Sis, take heed to the warnings now. Please don't wait to be seriously hurt before you realise that the barriers you thought were limiting you were actually protecting you. Please don't wait until it's too late before you realise you were better off being obedient to God than indulging in the temporary satisfaction of sin. You think you have all the time in the world to get right with God, to truly surrender your life to Him, but your days are numbered. You don't even know when your last day is, so why continue to take the risk? Know the Lord is coming back again, and the only reason why He hasn't yet is because He's being patient for our sakes. He doesn't want anyone lost to the world but wants everyone to repent. This is why He has given us more time (2 Peter 3:9).

As much as we don't like to think or talk about it, a day will come when each and every one of us will have to give an account of our lives to God (Romans 14:12). An ignorant sinner is one thing, but a wilful, intentional, habitual sinner who deliberately rebels against God even after receiving the full knowledge of the truth? (Luke 12: 48)

No matter what sin(s) you keep running back to, they will never be worth it when compared to the consequences, so please don't wait for another day to repent when tomorrow isn't promised. Seize this very moment and turn away from your sins by wholeheartedly turning to God. God tells us how to do this. He says: *If we confess our sins, he is faithful and just and will forgive us our sins and purify us from all unrighteousness. 1 John 1: 9 (NIV)*

Coming to God really is that easy. Confess your sins and repent and watch Him change you from the inside out. He desires to change you not because of who you are but because of who He is (Ephesians 2:8).

2) A Willing Heart:
<u>"And Solomon, my son, learn to know the God of your ancestors intimately. Worship and serve him with your whole heart and a willing mind. For the Lord sees every heart and knows every plan and thought. If you seek him, you will find him. But if you forsake him, he will reject you forever." - 1 Chronicles 28:9</u>

If you expect me to say that as soon as I gave my life to Christ life, as soon as I decided to be a fulfilled Singleton and not a frustrated one, that life got easier, I would be lying. Yes, eventually it did get easier, but see, society had conditioned me for years to act a certain way when hurt – to get closure on a relationship before moving on; to throw myself a constant pity party when I saw others around me happy and in relationships I longed to be in. So be under no illusion here – yes, relationships messed me up and damaged me, but I still longed to be in one because I felt more comfort in a relationship than out of one. I was the dog that unwisely returned to its vomit and the washed pig that foolishly returned to the mud (2 Peter 2:22).

In time however, I noticed a change from the woman I used to be to the woman I was becoming starting with a very flirtatious text received from *Mr. What Were You Thinking?* A message like that would have spurred me on to flirt back, but it was actually a reminder that I hadn't blocked him from contacting me, so I did exactly that. In that moment I realised I had gone from an insecure girl who used to get a man's attention any way possible to a woman only after God's attention. I went from being a girl who used to be consumed with jealousy of other people's relationships to being a woman who was only after a relationship with Christ. I went from being that girl who begged for any sense of security from others to a woman who only felt secure in God's presence. Did it happen overnight? Sorry, but no!

Healing is a process, and a process takes time. The problem is, we live in a world of quick fixes; we are a generation just not willing to wait. We are broken, damaged, and insecure. We've been in people bondage and soul ties for years and have no sense of self-worth. Yet if we don't feel better about our situation the minute we decide it's time to change, we end up jumping on a new quick fix. We end up going back to those dead end relationships with *Mr. I Don't Even Know Where I'm Going, So How Do I Lead You?* All because we are not willing to wait for God to work on us! If God wanted to change your situation today, He could, but then how would that bring Him glory? How would you appreciate how far you've come if you never travelled anywhere, and how would your testimony be a blessing to others?

So for all of you who are still reading and didn't put the book down when I laid myself bare in Chapter 2, know that in order to see change and be changed, God requires a willing participant. He can only work with someone who *wants* to change. Think of it like this: the most important *choice* you will ever have to make is that of salvation. So if God gives you free will regarding salvation, then why do you think He will force anything less on you?

I get it – your heart has been hardened, and you wonder why, years down the line you still can't forgive that cheating ex or that woman who 'stole your man,' but how long will you go on feeling like this?

I'll be honest: did I initially come to God with an unforgiving and unwilling heart? Absolutely! You read my story right? I had a hit list of people on my phone that I needed to track down and avenge in this lifetime! I told God how much I hated all the random dudes I had wasted my time on; I told Him that I better not catch any one of them alone because I would probably hurt them *(Jesus was probably like, "You and whose army?")*, and I pleaded with Him to let some of my exes get back in contact with me so I could lead them on the way they led me on and show them just how good I was doing without *them (even though that was a total lie at the time)*. But I also told God that I hated feeling the way that I did, that I was tired of constantly being angry and bitter and taking it out on those around me. I cried out to Him daily that although I hated them now, I wanted to reach a point in my life where I wished them all well, and guess what? God worked with that – He worked with an honest and willing heart.

So how do you come to God with a willing heart? It's simple; express to God exactly what it is you need starting with Him. Tell God how much you desire Him in your life. How desperate you are for a relationship with Him. How miserable and unhappy you are. How consumed you are with your ex that it hurts. Let God know you're jealous of those around you that seem to have everything you want. That being single feels like a curse, but you want to see the beauty in it. That you don't even desire marriage but deep down; you know it's because of the hurt and pain you've experienced over the years and not because of the gift He has bestowed upon you. Just be open and honest with Him by ushering Him into every area of your life. God knows exactly how you feel and what you harbour in your heart so nothing said will be a shock to Him. He does however want you to express yourself to Him. No matter how raw, undiluted or incomprehensible your feelings are; it doesn't matter: Just be real with Him any way you know how, and watch Him begin to work on you.

Every morning, and noon I cry out in distress, and He hears my voice. - Psalm 55:17

Our Heavenly Father has promised that when we cry out to Him, He hears us. It makes sense then that you should not waste your time complaining to those who cannot help and instead cry out to the only One who can.

3) Forgiveness:

It's your sins that have cut you off from God. Because of your sins, he has turned away and will not listen anymore. – Isaiah 59:2

You: *"All right, Lord, I'm ready and willing – change me!"*

Jesus: *"Let's start with forgiveness."*

You: *"Sorry, what?"*

Jesus: *"Let's start with forgiveness. Forgiving your ex who treated you badly, who left you to raise your child alone, who wasn't willing to commit even after 10 years together, who cheated on you throughout your relationship, who told you marriage wasn't for him but then married the next woman after you. Forgiving your absent father whom you measure all men to. Forgiving yourself for having that abortion, for staying with a guy longer than you should have. Let's deal with it.*

You: *"Nah, forget that!"*

I am a massive Candy Crush fan! Let me keep it real: I can be too tired to read my daily Bible plan, but never too tired of a game of Candy Crush! But for all you Candy Crush lovers, don't you just hate it when you've been stuck on a difficult level for days *(maybe even weeks – don't judge me!)*, and you've finally gotten through it *(yippee!!!!)* only for the next level to have a burgundy box pop up with the words *'hard level'* flash on your screen. *"So bruh, what was the level before known as?"* Yet you can't go unto the next level unless you've passed the current one. That's how a willing heart and forgiveness work. We've passed what we thought was a difficult level in willing God to change us, only to be hit with an actual tough level, 'forgiveness.' Yet if we don't forgive, we can't move on to the next phrase of the healing process.

Unforgiveness not only affects us as individuals but also robs us of an intimate relationship with Christ. Unforgiveness delays the full life God intended for us to have and also creates an opening for Satan to manoeuvre into our lives (2 Corinthians 2:5-11.) When we refuse to forgive others or even ourselves, our lips are saying, *"Lord, I'm a willing participant,"* but our actions are showing, *"but I won't submit to everything."* We know actions speak far louder than words, and God looks at the heart of man and not the lips of man. (1 Samuel 16:7). Therefore, how do you expect to see change in your life when you haven't wholeheartedly submitted it to God?

"Get rid of all bitterness, rage, anger, harsh words, and slander, as well as all types of evil behaviour. Instead, be kind to each other, tender-hearted, forgiving one another, just as God through Christ has forgiven you."- Ephesians 4:31-32

It took me twice as long to get over an ex just because I was unwilling to forgive him for the way he had treated me. *"All I want is an apology,"* was what I would tell myself when he came to mind, and I was full of anger and bitterness towards him. I felt the lack of closure on a long relationship, and no apology was hindering me from moving forward with my life, which only made me resent him even more.

By the time I gave my life to Christ, it had been 3 years since this particular dude and I had broken up, and yet I still loathed him like it had been just the other day. I could clearly see that I definitely wasn't holding his life back *(yes, I was that crazy ex that kept tabs on him!)*. So why was an apology I was clearly never going to receive holding me back? The reason was simple: I thought I needed the apology to move on, and because I hadn't received it, I couldn't forgive. Even after 3 years, this ex still had power over me, and I thought if only he would apologise/acknowledge he was wrong/at least try to act sorry, then I would find the strength and ability to forgive him and finally move on.

"Cursed are those who put their trust in mere humans, who rely on human strength and turn their hearts away from the Lord." – Jeremiah 17:5

"Don't put your confidence in powerful people; there is no help for you there." – Psalm 146:3

"Don't put your trust in mere humans. They are as frail as breath. What good are they?" – Isaiah 2:22

We struggle so much with forgiveness because we believe the offending party has a role to play in whether we forgive them or not. We think forgiveness and an apology go hand in hand, so if we don't receive one, then we can't do the other. Yet we fail to see that subconsciously not only are we relying on our own abilities to forgive, but also we are giving someone else ultimate power over the outcome of our lives. And you know what the crazy part is? That person has no idea! They have moved on with their lives; they have had multiple girlfriends since you, are maybe even married now, yet you are still stuck being a bitter jealous ex to a guy who most probably no longer gives you a second thought. You need to let go of the idea that forgiveness makes you weak or a doormat, that forgiveness means you excuse the offender's hurtful actions, that you can only forgive once you gain closure, or that forgiveness means the offending person will not suffer the consequences of their actions. Strive to get to a place where you are praying for those who have hurt you instead of cussing them out at the mention of their names. I got into the habit of praying for people who had hurt me (not *'may his punishment be swift and severe'* prayers, but, *'he wasn't great to me, but Lord, grant him the ability to know how to treat the next woman right'* prayers), and in time found it difficult to hate the very people I was praying for. What I didn't know at the time was that as I was praying for them, God was blessing me!

Praying for those who have hurt and mistreated you is hard and doesn't come naturally, but it is still the lifestyle we have been called by God to live (Luke 6: 27-28, Matthew 5:43-45). We are instructed to forgive with no exemptions or clauses. So even when some actions just seem unforgiveable, remember: forgiveness is not even for the other person; it is for you!

Forgiveness means that you set yourself free from the chains of bitterness and resentment and move on. If God doesn't hold you a prisoner of your past, why do allow men to? (And yes, you allow it. Forgiveness is a choice – you either choose to forgive somebody or you don't!) The truth is, you are not always going to get an apology. The guy who broke your heart and then the dude who came after and completely desecrated what was left are not always going to realise or sadly even care about how much damage they have caused. While you can choose to carry resentment and hatred in your heart and into new relationships, you can also choose to let God give you the strength to forgive. Granted, through your own strength and might, you may always struggle with this, but do you know what's so great about having the Holy Spirit reside in you? You don't have to do it alone – the Holy Spirit makes up for every area you lack.

For some, forgiving others is easy; it's forgiving ourselves that we struggle with. For a long time, I couldn't forgive myself for 'allowing' another person to take advantage of me. I didn't see myself as a victim of sexual abuse until years later and blamed myself for the ruined life I thought I was living. I couldn't forgive myself for being in a situation where my husband wouldn't be the first man I would sleep with. I couldn't forgive myself for the years wasted of just existing and never really living. I regarded myself as weak for even allowing life to get me so down that I had tried to end it and saw myself as a disappointment for being so fragile and pathetic.

I remember the first time I came across a Singleton's favourite Bible passage (1 Corinthians 13:4-8) and just mediating on it for months and months. It was on my phone screen saver, my Blackberry status, written all over my diary, and I would say to myself, *"The next man who comes into my life needs to love me like these verses state."* I recognized that these verses gave the true definition of love; the way we are loved by God and the love God expects us to show to others. I desired for my spouse to love me like this, but knew I needed to learn to love myself like this first because self-forgiveness starts with self-love.

I couldn't learn to forgive others while never learning to forgive myself. I couldn't demand a love that keeps no record of being wronged when I was constantly keeping a tally of every time I messed up. How would I even recognise a love that is kind, patient, and not rude when I was none of these things to Christina Tosin Fasoro? I had to learn to accept myself and my flaws and realise that my failings didn't make me less of a person but instead contributed to the person I am today. I made the choice to embark on a new path to growth and leave everything else behind me. My past is exactly that – the past – and incapable of being changed. My future, however – that is still worth something, or else the enemy wouldn't be trying so hard to interfere with it.

Today, I stand boldly with my head held high. I can freely admit that I haven't made the best choices in life, but I refuse to be held back by them. I let go of the things I cannot change and move on because I AM FREE! God in His sovereignty has promised to take the wasted years and restore them to good before it is all over (Joel 2:25), so what benefit is it to keep mulling over the former things?

Beautiful beloved woman of God: Do you know what your Heavenly Father see's when He looks at you? He doesn't see sin or your past mistakes; Instead, He sees the perfection of Christ (Hebrews 10:17, Romans 5:5, Ephesians 4:24.) So instead of seeing yourself through the eyes of hurt, betrayal, imperfection and disappointment; see yourself through the eyes of the Lord. See yourself as perfection because the Greater One lives within you.

4) End toxic relationships

"Don't be fooled by those who say such things, for bad company corrupts good character."

- 1 Corinthians 15:33

I am a hoarder! I've got study materials from years (I mean *years*) ago. I've got birthday and Christmas cards from years (I mean *years*) ago, and I still have clothes that don't fit, have never fitted, and will probably never fit me, but I still keep them because I just can't bear to throw them away. Oh, and I used to be a hoarder of men as well! Even after I got saved, I still entertained guys I had no business whatsoever entertaining because there was nobody that couldn't be put to good use! I kept on thinking, *"Just in case this Christian thing doesn't work out for me, I need Mr. Flavour of the Month and Mr. Indifferent to run back to."* Not only did my actions show a total lack of faith in God, but it deeply hindered my spiritual growth because God desired for me to be on such a higher level of faith then I was. However, my heart was so overcrowded with crap that I had no space to manoeuvre anywhere.

I remember a particular evening when I found myself in a room surrounded by great women of God. They were sharing their testimonies on how God clearly spoke to them, moved in miraculous ways in their lives, and how they had a personal encounter with Him. I remember just sitting down almost in tears and saying to myself, *"God, I want that. I want the same intimacy with you as these women have. Don't I deserve such a relationship?"* Yet even in the midst of my jealousy, ever so quietly, the Holy Spirit spoke to me on how much He desired intimacy with me. He reminded me of the many times I had sat down at my quiet place with my Bible wide open, pen in my hand, and ready to get filled with His word. Then a random guy would call or text me, and instantly, I no longer desired to spend time with Him because it seemed something better had come along. He reminded me how passionately I used to pray about my heart no longer aching after being broken yet again by another dude and how I would fall to my knees begging God for the pain to go away, and yet nowadays, I couldn't even get through a coherent prayer without drifting off to sleep. I didn't desire God and wondered why I was in spiritual stagnation all because I had made other relationships around me my god. I had a male 'friend' *(you know the sorts of friends I'm talking about!)* who I only entertained because nobody else was showing me interest. I had another 'friend' who gave me money and brought me stuff because he thought he would get something particular in return (that 'friend' never did). I had another 'friend' who was a yes man and boasted my confidence by constantly showering me with compliments. So what room was there for God when my actions showed that I didn't need Him because my needs were seemingly being met by these poor guys I was stringing along and abusing?

I know some of you may be thinking, *"Christina! Giiiirl! That's not abuse! I have friends like that too!"* But listen up: When you are able to manipulate a guy to do things for you because he is under the illusion that you are something more than you really are, that's abuse. When you continually lead a guy on that you have no interest in and he brings something (materialistic or otherwise) to the table, it's abuse. It is wrong, shameful, and you need to stop it! Why do think it's ok to treat people this way? It is not ok to only speak to *Mr. Fresh of The Boat* when you want a great night out that you have no intention of paying for! How dare you be angry at God for not bringing you a great guy when you use and abuse the great guys in your life! If you have no interest in them, cut them off (nicely) so that they can be with a woman who is interested!

Understand our God is a jealous God (Exodus 20:5), so just a part of you won't do; He desires **all of you.** No love on this earth will ever measure up to the love God has for you, so why are you so determined to acquire the love of a man, and thereby making him an idol, when it is God who loves you unconditionally and is the reason you are still standing today?

Ending toxic relationships isn't gender specific; you can be in toxic relationships with females too. Yes, your ride or die, your day1, your bestie, gal from waaay back when, are all great people, I'm sure, but some friendships are poisonous and are hindering your spiritual growth. An innocent dinner date with your gal pals turns into an evening of gossip galore without you even realising it because you're a new creation still trying to fit the mould of your old self even though the two can't coincide! (2 Corinthians 5:17)

I recall a particular evening after work when my girlfriends and I decided to catch up over dinner. But before I knew it, the conversation had taken an unexpected turn and went from 0 to 100 reaaaal quick! I felt so embarrassed and just sat there like the prude I have become. Anyway, as I was leaving the restaurant, the Holy Spirit asked me how I represented Him among my friends. I was actually feeling quite pleased with myself. I was like, *"Really well, actually. Even when the conversation turned sexual, I didn't participate at all. I just sat there lost for words. Did you catch my stunned expressions, Daddy?"* The Lord then said to me, *"But that conversation made you want to reach out to an ex because you felt like you were missing something. That conversation didn't glorify me whatsoever; it glorified pre- marital sex, and your silence condoned it. You didn't tell them the conversation was making you uncomfortable or ask that they talk about something else. Don't you know that you are meant to be a witness to these very people?"* Welp! That certainly put me in my place that evening!

The thing is, it might seem like just an *innocent* conversation, just an *innocent* place to go, or just an *innocent* friendship, but what you are actually doing is planting a seed. You're feeding your flesh and starving the Spirit. In the battle against our flesh and the Spirit, who do you think wins? The flesh gets the victory all because you let this and that slide, you didn't check that friendship, you entertained questionable conversations, and you didn't guard your heart! (Proverbs 4:23)

Accepting that some friendships will inevitably come to an end is a bitter pill to swallow. When I got serious in my walk with Christ, I lost a lot of friends; however, out of all the relationships that ended, none of them were because I made a public declaration to cut off the friendship. They would invite me to a club, and I would tell them I no longer went clubbing as I had to be vigilant of the places I was going and the kind of music I would be listening to. They would invite me to a drink or to smoke Hookah, and I would politely decline, telling them that I no longer put just anything in my body. It got to a point where the texts and phone calls to go out and do certain things stopped rolling in because they knew it would be a resounding "no" from me. I was quickly known as the 'kill-joy', the 'grandma', the 'too Christian,' and the 'boring member' of the group. I gradually stopped receiving texts and phone calls altogether. I realised the places I was going, they weren't going, and I was fine with that. They weren't holding me back, and I wasn't spoiling their 'fun,' so it was a win win! So while some friendships may require a public declaration to that individual that your friendship has run its course (in which you need to pray for the Holy Spirit to lead you in this area), I believe most will simply just melt away because your actions *should* speak for themselves as to whose standards you have chosen to follow.

5) Be filled with the beautiful things of the Lord
"Guard your heart above all else, for it determines the course of your life." – Proverbs 4:23

Question time, ladies: What happens when you take out your favourite heels or Converses from their box? Or take away just one nail polish from the rest of your collection? *Drumroll, please*………………………!!!!! The answer is……………………….. It leaves a space! And the same thing happens in our personal lives as well. We cut off *Mr. Lack of Respect*, stop watching garbage TV shows, and stop entertaining questionable conversations only to find ourselves back with *Mr. Lack of*

Respect, sitting in front of the TV watching programmes we know are no good and talking recklessly with others while apologising to God (*in our head*) every other sentence. Why? Because we've created a space from the activities we used to do and because we don't know how to spend our newfound time, we find ourselves running back to mess we don't even like!

If you know me well, you know that I used to have a massive addiction to gossip websites (even after I got saved!). I wouldn't go a day without catching up with all the juicy goss from the last 24 hours and would spend hours fixated on which celebrity broke up with whom or which celebrity was sleeping with whom. So one evening, the Lord laid it on my heart that He wanted me to fast – and not just an ordinary fast; He wanted me to abstain from literally everything. Not just food and drink, but also gossip websites, worldly music, ungodly television programmes and conversations for the duration of my 21-day fast.

Day 2 into the fast, and I was already thinking that this *"abstain from everything thing"* really wasn't going to work out for me. My hour lunch break that I would have spent reading 4 different gossip websites, I instead spent staring at my blank computer screen in despair. In the evening, as I was breaking my fast, I would eat in complete silence because I was now at a loss for what to watch. By day 5, I had substituted my ruthless, cutthroat gossip sites for gossip sites not as savage but still *'ouch'* to the person they were slagging off. I was watching TV programmes that did not glorify God, but according to me, did not persuade me to act ungodly either, and yet, I didn't feel good about it. I knew it was unpleasing to the Lord, and I had come to the realisation of just how trashy and impressionable worldly media really is. Yet, I couldn't escape it because there was no positive substitute for the space I had created in my heart for the negative things I was used to.

One night, after some serious and heartfelt prayer, I was expectant that God would get me through the next 14 days of the fast, and sure enough, He did! Instead of jumping on my favourite entertainment site at lunchtime, the Lord instructed me to read Christian blogs and go out for a walk while listening to gospel music. Instead of listening to my favourite Afrobeats artist whose lyrics are sometimes....urm....... somethingish, I instead substituted it for African praise, and still got my giggle on *(shout out, Midnight Crew!)*. And instead of watching garbage TV programmes, I used the time to watch sermons, read Christian books, and write! It actually began a healthy addiction that even after my fast came to an end, I no longer found myself craving the things I used to.

Let's be real with ourselves: How many of us have gotten out of unhealthy relationships only to find ourselves missing *Mr. Unfaithful* at particular times of the day so much (usually the time we would speak to him most) that we end up returning one of his many messages all because of the void left behind? How many of us dread Valentine's Day or are so miserable on what would have been our x year(s) anniversary that we spend the whole day mopping about? Reaching out instead to *Mr. Always Available* for comfort? How many of us have turned to watching porn? Having purely sexual relationships because we still crave sexual satisfaction? How many of us need alcohol in our bloodstream, nicotine flowing through our lungs, or being intoxicated with other drugs to have a good time or get through the day, because without it, nothing else cheers us up? How many of us have learned to stop bashing others, but the comments section on a gossip website or Instagram page is still our favourite place to go because we take pleasure in seeing others bash the people we would like to?

You see, the desire to get laid doesn't just go away just because *Mr. Unfaithful* does. Knowing you shouldn't reach out to an ex doesn't mean you won't, and being told that alcohol and drugs are damaging to your health doesn't mean you stop indulging in them. There comes a time when we want to stop doing these very things but keep going back to them all because we've created a space in our hearts to do them. When we do stop doing them, a void is left. The emptiness has to be filled with something, and because it is not being filled with the beautiful things of the Lord, another master fills it with what our carnal self still desires.

Apostle Paul is that Guy! Don't get me wrong, in real life, Jesus is my bestie, but in my head, Apostle Paul is a very close friend because he always kept it real. He acknowledged that even as Christians, although we want to do what's right and obey God, our sinful flesh refuses to respond to His law:

<u>"What I don't understand about myself is that I decide one way, but then I act another, doing things I absolutely despise. So if I can't be trusted to figure out what is best for myself and</u>

then do it, it becomes obvious that God's command is necessary. But I need something more! For if I know the law but still can't keep it, and if the power of sin within me keeps sabotaging my best intentions, I obviously need help! I realize that I don't have what it takes. I can will it, but I can't do it. I decide to do good, but I don't really do it; I decide not to do bad, but then I do it anyway. My decisions, such as they are, don't result in actions. Something has gone wrong deep within me and gets the better of me every time. It happens so regularly that it's predictable. The moment I decide to do good, sin is there to trip me up. I truly delight in God's commands, but it's pretty obvious that not all of me joins in that delight. Parts of me covertly rebel, and just when I least expect it, they take charge. I've tried everything and nothing helps. I'm at the end of my rope. Is there no one who can do anything for me? Isn't that the real question? The answer, thank God, is that Jesus Christ can and does. He acted to set things right in this life of contradictions where I want to serve God with all my heart and mind, but am pulled by the influence of sin to do something totally different." - Romans 7:14-25 (MSG)

In spite of the ever present war between our flesh and spirt, Apostle Paul offers the only solution to this problem which is Jesus.

Understand that you don't overcome the craving of pre-marital sex by indulging in it; neither do you get over an ex by keeping him around until you're ready to let go. Instead, you **SURROUND, IMMERSE** and **BURY** yourself in Jesus by studying His word and spending time with Him. You can't begin to hate what He hates and love what He loves when you don't even know what He hates and loves. The more consumed you are with the things of the Lord, the less you desire anything that is not of Him.

6) Renew your mind:
<u>Don't copy the behaviour and customs of this world, but let God transform you into a new person by changing the way you think. Then you will learn to know God's will for you, which is good and pleasing and perfect.</u> – Romans 12: 2

So I've recently had some health issues. According to the doctors, it will be difficult for me to naturally conceive *(yet I can't wait to share this testimony of when I have children one day!)*. When I first heard the news however, I was so upset. I have never been so down in my Christian walk, started suffering from depression again, and if I can be completely honest, was upset with God. Just when I thought everything in my life was starting to come together and I could handle whatever was thrown at me, this came along and shook me. I knew what I needed to do (seek comfort in my Father's arms), but I instead distanced myself from Him, allowing the enemy to creep in and wreak havoc in my life. The enemy reminded me of my past and that I've done some pretty bad stuff, so this was punishment for it all. He convinced me I was damaged goods and no man would want me because I had so much baggage and would struggle to have kids. I have some pretty amazing friends (thank God for godly friendships!) who didn't allow me to wallow in self-pity, who blatantly told me *"so what"* concerning the doctors' reports, and who prayed for me when I couldn't even pray for myself. Now, I can't wait for the day where I roll up to my doctor's office, baby bump in tow, and be like, *"What were you saying that time, doc?"*

The doctor's report remains the same concerning my health, but I don't live my life by it. When I first heard the news, I was looking at it from a worldly perspective and reacted how my flesh processed the news. Now, I look at it from God's prospective. I live in confidence knowing that even if man, nature, or science says no; my Father's YES is all that matters. I live by absolute faith, nothing else. If my Father desires it for me, then so it will be, and that's that!

So the question is, how do you see yourself? Do you see yourself as incomplete because you are single? Do you view yourself as unloved because nobody is currently showing you attention? Do you think that your heart's desires will never come into existence because of your past mistakes? Do you believe you will never have kids because you had an abortion when you were younger? Do you think that nobody wants you because you've grown up feeling like a burden to everyone else? Do you think you've passed your prime of settling down? Do you believe you're destined to remain miserable and single? Do you think because you're a single mother no guy is going to want you? Do you think God hates you and won't bless you just because you're divorced? Do you know that all these thoughts don't just go away because you have given your life to Christ?

Being a Christian means more than avoiding worldly behaviour. It's more than exchanging one master for another and so much more than replacing worldly do's and don'ts for godly ones. Truly experiencing God and finding fulfilment in every season involves not only conforming to God's word but being transformed by it also. God understands that as Christians, we are still in the world (although not of it), but He desires for us to view the world from His perspective and not ours. He doesn't want us crushed by our own negative thoughts, feelings, or by what we see going on with our limited sight. He wants us to view everything the way He does. He wants our lives to change and reflect His nature and character. He wants His attitudes to become our attitudes, His desires to become our desires, what He hates to become what we hate, and what He loves to be what we love also. He wants us to replace our worldly knowledge, logic, and rationalisation with His truth. Yet the only way we can retrain our minds to the truth is to know the truth (John 8:32).

The truth is found in reading and studying the word of God and spending time at the feet of the author. You are perfect in God's sight, and through Him, you are made whole. There is no such thing as 'too late' or damaged goods with Him. You are a masterpiece to your Creator, and anyone else who thinks or says differently is a LIAR! That negative voice in your head is a LIE, and you need to train your mind and thoughts to think the truth: the reality of God instead of the illusion of the world and think in line with the spirit and not the flesh. With a renewed mind, you get to experience every season with joy and the understanding that it is needed to propel you to the next season. Only with a renewed mind can you go from a struggling Singleton to a content one.

7) Know who you are in Christ
"This means that anyone who belongs to Christ has become a new person. The old life is gone; a new life has begun!"– 2 Corinthians 5:17

To most people, I'm known as Christina, but when my mum gave birth to me, she named her beautiful chubby baby girl Oluwatosin Fasoro *(+ 5 other names - you know how some African parents do!)*. Christina was the name given to me by my uncle and my middle name; however, when the rumours started about me during secondary school, I would purposely hang out in areas where nobody knew me and go by the name Christina. I legally changed my name to Christina Tosin Fasoro a few years later. Now with pride I tell people both my names. I'm unconcerned with which name someone prefers to call me because I'm unashamed of my past, and I embrace my roots. Yet at the time, the name Tosin was a constant reminder of persistent and untrue rumours about me. It was a constant reminder of the 'weak' girl that was taken advantage of and abused, and was a constant reminder of the weak and messed up person I saw myself as. So I found comfort in people knowing me solely as Christina, because then I could pretend to be a totally different person without my name and the past associated with it speaking for me. Regardless of what area I found myself in and the name I chose to go by, internally I was still the same Tosin as I was Christina, and vice versa.

The truth is, we all have pasts, we've all made mistakes and suffered the consequences for them, yet we continue to beat ourselves up over things we simply cannot change. We have become so disgusted with ourselves, with the choices that we've made, or even our physical appearance that we make every effort to fix ourselves externally and seek everyone else's approval, attention, and applause. Internally, however, we are wrecks. We're so ashamed and frustrated with the person we are that we become slaves to our own past, unable to break free all because we fail to understand how beautiful we are in the eyes of God who doesn't judge our pasts but instead promises us better futures.

See, when you surrender your life to Christ, your old life, regardless of the person you used to be, is **NO MORE**. Your past no longer has to dictate your future because you are now a new creation and one with Christ (Galatians 2:20). You don't need to live your life based on the labels and stereotypes other people have given you. You don't need to be the person society expects you to be, your family is pushing you to be, or the person your ex wanted you to be. You are now given the strength and ability to become the woman God foreordained you to be. Your past is exactly that – your past – and you don't have to continue to live in its shadow. Let go of all previous labels and stereotypes and allow God to mask you with new ones.

In the past, you may have been labelled all kind of things and regardless of whether they were true or not, you believed them. Yet the person you are in Christ, the person God has transformed you into, and the person you ought to see yourself as, should be completely opposite to the person you used to be without Him in your life. You can't allow people who don't even know you tell you who you are! (And that includes you! People who know who they are do not speak negativity towards themselves.) If your views of yourself are distorted and you can't trust them; remember your Creator knows exactly who He created. All you need to do is return back to the Source to figure out your identity. It's like when you're trying to put together a new chest of draws and you don't know the next step, you go back the instructions given by the manufacturer to help you out. Our walk with God is no different. In His word, you WILL find yourself. You will see that you are apple of your Father's eye and perfect in His sight.

Here are a few other promises I discovered, and as Daughters of Christ, they apply to us all!

- ❖ We our greatly loved (Ephesians 2:4).

- ❖ We are deeply cared for (Philippians 4:6-7)

- ❖ The penalty for our sins has been paid, and we have been forgiven (Isaiah 53:5).

- ❖ We can now stand unashamed, as we are free from all condemnation (Romans 8:1).

- ❖ We are delivered from the power and clutches of darkness (Colossians 1:13).

❖ We are set free from the past and accepted as our Father's very own (Ephesians 1:7).

❖ We are no longer alone, for the Greater One lives within us (1 John 4:4).

❖ We are overcomers (Revelation 12:11).

❖ There is nothing that we cannot do through Christ Jesus who strengthens us (Philippians 4:13).

❖ We lack nothing (Philippians 4:19).

❖ We do not need a husband or a group of friends to complete us; we are already complete (Colossians 2:10).

❖ We are ambassadors for Christ, and in Him our identity is found (2 Corinthians 5:20).

Understand that you are all the above and so much more! We have been created in our perfect Father's image (Genesis 1:27) and although God is a spirit and does not have a form like us, He created us to have mental, spiritual, and emotional characteristics that reflect His own. So if you're struggling in this area, how about you find your identity in Christ and His word rather than in what people say you are or even in who you think you are?

8) Set Biblical standards
"Study this book of the law continually. Mediate on it day and night so you will be sure to obey everything written in it. Only then will you prosper and succeed in all you do. This is my command – be strong and courageous! Do not be afraid or discouraged. For the Lord your God is with you wherever you go." – Joshua 1:8-9

Let me make this point crystal clear; YOU CANNOT TAKE RELATIONSHIP ADVICE FROM UNBELEIVERS! It does not matter that their relationship is flourishing, that she got the ring in a year, or that he shows her off for the world to see; they do not operate the way you have been called to! You do not see what internal struggle they have to go through, what ungodly sacrifices they have to make to maintain the relationship and the insecurities of being in an ungodly relationship brings. You're accepting advice from people who are of the world and not of God. These people tell you that a man respects you more if you wait until at least the third date to give it up, when God has commanded you to wait until you are pronounced husband and wife (Hebrews 13: 4.) You think it's ok to dress scanty because a worldly chick tells you that's one of the ways to 'keep a man' even though God has called us all to modest dressing (1 Timothy 2:8-10.) And then you wonder why your relationships never work out when you're using ungodly rules and behaviours to build a godly relationship.

When you understand who you are in Christ, your standards change to reflect God's. Instead of being interested in what social media define as 'relationship goals,' you're only concerned about the standard God sets. You understand that marriage is a ministry as well as singleness and qualities that may have made the cut before just won't do it now. You desire for yourself what God desires for you, and your goal isn't just to get married but to be a helpmeet to your husband, to be one with your husband, to compliment your husband and love him the way you are loved by God. The problem is, many of us don't understand this because even when we become saved, our standards are based on everything else but the word of God. We watch the way others live their lives – even Christians – and base our standards off what we glimpse from their social media pages and the little we know of them.

God's word is clear: He says "study the word continually" (Joshua 1: 8-9), not study Pastor so and so or BlackBeauty&Brains from Instagram *(I don't know if that person actually exists – no shade if they do!).* Even this very book you're reading: it is not to be taken as the Gospel, neither is it an extension, addition, or replacement for the Bible. It is your responsibility to make sure it matches up with what God says and not blindly follow because it's written by someone claiming to be a Christian *(although I really am – but you get my point!)*

From the lifestyle you live to the spouse you desire, make sure you set biblical standards, or you will blow just like the wind does. Don't fall victim to the lies of the enemy that tell you your standards are too high and that's why you're still single, that there are not enough Christian men in the church so you need to look outside the church, or if you would only dress a little less "Little House On The Prairie" and a little more "Baywatch," then guys would at least look your way. If your standards are biblical and based on personal conviction, then nothing else matters and God will surely provide your heart's desire (Psalm 37:4.)

Do you know one of the beautiful things about this season? You have the time to figure out who you are and what God desires for your future. In knowing this, you protect yourself from a lot of heartbreak. You understand that not every good looking Christian brother in your church is the guy for you. His purpose of traveling the world to preach might not align with your purpose of setting up a local business. He might want 5 kids while you anticipate stopping after 2. He might not even want kids, while your life wouldn't be complete without them.

As a single woman, don't be so fixated on the moment you become a wife that you disregard the precious time leading up to it. If you won't submit to God, why do you think you will submit to your husband? If you have no ambition or vision, why do you crave a spouse with exactly those qualities? If you are prayer starving, how can you desire a spouse prayer hungry? Don't be so concerned about your outer attributes that you don't even pay attention to your inner ones. Yes, a curvalicious body and luscious lips may be pleasing to the eye, but that doesn't help when you begin to notice a disconnect between you and your husband. Being a social butterfly won't assist you when the enemy starts attacking your children and staying ahead of the fashion game won't help when the Holy Spirit prods you in the middle of the night to pray for someone under attack. Don't be so concerned about your external that your internal life holds no substance.

Let's be honest with ourselves: some of us are not single because God has forgotten about us or because we are underserving of a spouse. We're single because we are just not ready to be with someone else. Instead of us using this season to grow closer to the Lord, letting Him mould us into His image and purge out bad habits, we allow resentfulness and hurt towards Him to grow in our hearts when He's just doing what any loving Father would – holding back things we just aren't ready for.

Appreciate this time to immerse yourself in the word of God. Listen to sermons on marriage, the role of a godly wife, and the role of a godly husband. Attend relationship/marriage seminars at church even when you're still single. Utilise the women in your church who are married and gain understanding from them (just make sure whatever they say aligns with the word of God.) Understand that marriage is not about no longer being lonely and having legitimate thighs in your bed; marriage is a ministry for God's glory. So be clear about what you're getting into and what is expected of you before you actually get into it.

9) *Learn To Trust God!*
"For I know the plans I have for you," says the LORD. "They are plans for good and not for evil, to give you a future and a hope." - Jeremiah 29:11

Learning to trust God simply means that you believe that God is good for you, has the power to help you, He loves you more than enough and will never give you or put you through something you can't handle.

Last year Christmas, I had a terrible toothache on the right side of my mouth. Now, if you've ever had problems with your teeth, I'm pretty sure you know how bad the pain can really be! I was in absolute agony, but I refused to go to the dentist. A couple of weeks prior to the pain, I had spent nearly £800 on the same tooth fixing it because of a dental procedure that went wrong (*my love of sweets also didn't help the matter.*) Anyway, I had spent all that money fixing the darn tooth, and I was still in pain, so the last place I wanted to go was back to the dentist! I spent Christmas day popping antibiotics and strong paracetamol, but nothing eased the pain. After I had run out of 'earthly options,' I thought, *'Oh, this would be a great opportunity to grow my faith,'* so I put away the antibiotics and paracetamol and waited for divine healing.

As I waited for God to heal me, I was in more pain then I've ever been and even cried myself to sleep a few times because of the throbbing and agonising ache in my mouth. I tried anointing oil, shouted, *"BY HIS STRIPES I AM HEALED"* x3, but nothing worked, and 'coincidently,' I started getting pain from a random tooth on the left side of my mouth as well. I was crying out to God for healing, but the pain just kept getting worse. By this stage, the pain was so severe that my right ear popped and started bleeding due to the pain, and my jaw was also on fire (not literally of course). In spite of all this, I knew that going to the dentist wasn't an option. I had reached the point where I was determined that if God didn't heal me, then I would be in pain for the rest of my life. Jesus was my dentist, so if He didn't heal me, then nobody/nothing else could.

Trusting God started out as running out of every other option, but eventually I truly believed God would work this miracle in my life. A few days later, when I had gone way beyond my pain threshold, the pain eased just a little bit. A day after that, the pain had eased even more, and within 4 days, the pain had totally gone. No painkillers, no dentist, no Google suggestions, but all from trusting Jesus. Here and there, I would feel a tingling sensation, an ache on the same tooth, and I would say to myself, *'Do you know how much pain I've been in before? This is nothing!'* I also knew that God had done it before: Not just in Bible stories or in anyone else's life, but now in my life, so there was no reason why He couldn't do it again. I have believed this ever since and have been healed ever since.

<u>Trust in the LORD with all your heart; do not depend on your own understanding.</u>

- Proverbs 3:5

Like my tooth situation, some of us learn to trust God, only when every other option has been exhausted. By this time we simply have no choice. Some of us have faced so many disappointments in our lives that we've learnt to only depend on ourselves. The thought of depending on anyone else scares us, but only God can say, *'trust me,'* and with complete confidence, we can, because He won't ever let us down (Psalm 9:10).

There is a benefit to trusting God in this single season, (even if the basis for your trust is because you have tried everything else and have no other option.) God is so amazing though, that in spite of this; He will make you see that He is the only option.

I know sometimes it doesn't make sense to trust God but understand there are benefits to trusting Him. Peace that only comes when you've left the matter in His hands. Divine strength that is only attainable when you've given your problems to the God bigger than your problems, and the certainty of experiencing God's presence, provisions and promises. The more you learn to trust Him, the less you worry about the 'unexpected' because you understand there's nothing you face alone. God will show you time and time again that He not only faces things *with* you but *for* you also. So beautiful beloved woman of God, will you trust God in your current situation?

10) Stop waiting and start living!

"*I want you to be free from the concerns of this life. An unmarried man can spend his time doing the Lord's work and thinking how to please him. But a married man has to think about his earthly responsibilities and how to please his wife. His interests are divided. In the same way, a woman who is no longer married or has never been married can be devoted to the Lord and holy in body and in spirit. But a married woman has to think about her earthly responsibilities and how to please her husband.*" - 1 Corinthians 7:32-34

There is so much beauty and personal growth that can be discovered in this season you're in! When your focus is solely on the Lord, when you find pleasure sitting at His feet and crave a relationship with your Maker, He will change your life around and reveal to you not only the great qualities that He has given you, but the not so great ones you picked up along the way that He needs to free you from in preparation for the next season of your life.

Learn to serve the Lord wholeheartedly and not because of what He can do for you but because of who He is. Learn to love this season, because the truth is, there are just some things that can only be learnt in this season in preparation for the next one. You can't appreciate the win if there was never a possibility of loss, and you can't appreciate the victory if you never even fought. Marriage is no different: you can't appreciate the beauty of being with anyone else when you can't even appreciate the beauty of being by yourself.

Life as a Singleton is beautiful, mysterious, and adventures, and you do not need to wait for a spouse to realise that. Get out of people bondage. You don't need a group of girls or a male companion to do stuff with. If a film you really want to see is out in cinema or a theatre production nobody else is interest in, go take your fine behind and go watch it. You don't need to wait for *Mr. But He Offered To Pay!* I love my dates with the Lord. When *we* go to the cinema, He reminds me that I'm not going to finish (*neither can I afford*) to get popcorn, sweets, and a Slush Puppy all at the same time. He always recommends that I go to the early afternoon viewings so I don't leave room for jealousy when I see other couples loved up and canoodling.

And when people think it's ok to talk throughout the film, He lets me know that I'm wasting my time cutting my eyes at them in the dark and kissing my teeth because they can't hear or see me!

If you like the way a diamond ring looks on your finger, buy yourself a purity ring and wear it on your wedding finger if that suits you. Stop telling yourself all the things you want to do now but are unable to do because you have no man, and just go out and do them by yourself or with your loved ones instead (with the obvious exceptions, of course.)

When we move into the next season of our lives, let us look back at this season with confidence that we achieved all we needed to. Let's enjoy our singleness because it's time we will never get back. Being single was never designed to be restrictive; it was designed to be liberating, so enjoy it!

Chapter 4

How About You Heal First?

Ok, bear with me here because I promise I'm going somewhere with this. I am definitely no psychologist, but from what the Lord has laid on my heart and based on personal observation, there are 2 types of <u>*hurt single females*</u> I have come across: the '***Nobody Wants Me***' type of woman and the '***Why Me***' type of woman.

The '*Nobody Wants Me*' type.

Aka 'The Settler'

The '*Nobody Wants Me*' type of woman is the woman who feels undesired because she's still single. She has welcomed in and made space in her heart for the voices in her head that tell her that her pickings are small – that she's not attractive enough, skinny enough, curvy enough, thin enough, sexy enough, black enough, white enough, light enough, rich enough, smart enough, popular enough, Christian enough, and whatever else 'enough,' so settles with whatever comes along.

The 'Nobody Wants Me' type of woman thinks she can bend, mould, and shape any guy to be the kind of guy she desires. The 'Nobody Wants Me' type of woman thinks she can bend, mould, and shape herself to be the kind of woman men seem attracted to. The 'Nobody Wants Me' type of woman walks around with this constant fear that she's never going to find anyone to settle down with.

The *'Why me'* type.

Aka *'The Unbothered'*

The *'Why me'* type of woman is the woman who has had to deal with heartbreak after heartbreak and who looks back at past relationships with bitterness, anger, and resentment. She often wonders, *why me*? Why did I have to go through what I went through? Why did I have to fall for *Mr. Problematic*? Why was I lied to? Why was I cheated on? Why was I so trusting? Why did I take him back after the last time? Why was I too loyal? Why was I this and why was he that? To stop her from further heartbreak, she either puts up walls impossible for any guy to get through or gives up on men altogether.

You with me so far?

If you're a hurt, single woman: regardless of what (if any) group you identify with, what tends to happen is that *Mr. Interested* begins to show interest *(would Mr. Interested do anything else?)*, and although he doesn't 'wow' you, you continue to entertain him because he's an option, he's available, and he's safe. *Mr. Pure Intentions* breaks through that strong barrier you always have up or begins to chip at your ice-cold heart. Although he ticks all the boxes, something just seems off. You can't explain it, describe it, or even put your finger on it, but these guys seem to be exactly what you've been looking for, yet you still feel unfulfilled. You often catch yourself examining your situation like, *"Is this it?"* So you either break things off, move the relationship up a notch, or jump from one guy to the next, thinking that will change everything.

While being distracted in a relationship, or busy getting to know a guy, you fail to notice that all these things distract you from..... well, *you*! You forget the time you were suffering from loneliness because someone's now offering you companionship. You can't remember having no sense of purpose because a new relationship has given you validity, and gone are the days of feeling insecure because your new man feeds your ego. Unconsciously, the guy is plastering over the cracks in your life, yet with all cracks; in time they begin to show. They begin to pierce through, all because you never dealt with the root cause of your loneliness, your behaviour, your insecurity, and your hurt. Inevitably the relationship/getting to know the guy stage breaks down, leaving you feeling more hurt, rejected, undesired, and even more closed off than before until another guy enters your life and the cycle begins again.

It seems to be everyone's fault but yours. It's God's fault: '*Why did He allow the relationship to even begin?*' It's the world's fault: '*Because there are no great men in your society,*' and it's the guy's fault: '*He didn't love you enough, care for you enough, spoil you enough, wasn't saved enough, didn't listen enough,'* etc. But the truth is, you just weren't healed enough. You weren't healed from your past, and instead of allowing God to heal you, mould you, rebuild, and restore you; you find yourself with what you thought you desired, yet still miserable. You find yourself accepting situations that in hindsight are so unlike you to accept.

This is not to blame it all on women and take away from the fact that there are a few men out there who are really wolves in sheep's clothing. – who pretend to be someone they're not for something they want; who 'pop up' in your life when you really weren't interested in a relationship, or through no fault of your own, lie, cheat, degrade, and treat you like crap. But for some of us, if we weren't so desperate for a relationship to begin with, we would have picked up on the signs early on. If we weren't so concerned about putting up a front, keeping up with a lifestyle or an ideology that really doesn't exist, we would have removed ourselves from bad situations time ago. If we were so secure in being single and trusting God's timing, a lot of guys would have never made it past *"hello."* No condemning, no judgement (*I've been that chick one to many times*), but just the truth.

So, how do you break the never-ending cycle you find yourself in with men? How do you heal? Simply put, you embrace being alone. (Note I said, *'embrace being alone,'* not embrace being lonely.) Loneliness can have a negative impact on your mental health (and I've talked on how to deal with loneliness in chapter 1,) whereas being alone can lead to the opposite effect. Being alone is a very fulfilling place to be. It's a state where you are always and constantly delighted in yourself, where you get to do things by yourself and for yourself and a place that gives room for God to work not only on you but with you as well.

You don't try to heal while being in a relationship or while trying to catch the attention of *Mr. Smart & Saved* because hurt people hurt people who then hurt people because they've been hurt *(did you catch that the first time?)*.

Any married person will tell you that marriage comes with its own set of trials and tribulations. Marriage is a reflection of each person in it and therefore reveals certain traits you didn't even know you had. Yet now as a single chick, you're aware that you have major trust issues, you're immature, insecure, suffer from low self-esteem, constantly suspicious, have problems with lust, still not over your ex, and will do anything for attention. Yet with all this in mind, you still get into something that should have been beautiful and pure but has now turned into one of the worst mistakes of your life. You need to heal from your pain BEFORE you entertain a new relationship, because even if he is the 'perfect guy,' he can't heal you. Sis, it's not even his job to! It's the job of your Heavenly Father, who actually desires to heal your broken heart and make you whole again (Psalms 147:3), so stop delegating God's work to mere mortals (Isaiah 2:22).

Some of you need healing from your sexual history, past relationships, a dysfunctional family life, sexual, physical and/or emotional abuse; the negative way you view yourself, and many other scars that have been inflicted on you over the years. Don't let the opportunity to deal with all of these issues now pass you by. The truth is, even if you refuse to deal with them now, you will inevitably have to deal with them later, and when another person is involved. Is it really fair for a great guy to have to deal with additional baggage that you should never have brought into the relationship in the first place? Is it even fair on yourself to delay issues you will unavoidably have to deal with to have a healthy relationship in the future? Time itself isn't a healer. It's what you do within that time that heals.

So how do you identify the issues you need to heal from?

The healing process I personally had to go through (*and in some areas am still going through*) was no walk in the park. I had been a Christian for a while, had forgiven and moved on, wasn't entertaining a guy so had no issues on that front, was obsessed and content with Jesus, and there was nothing known to me that I was hurting from and therefore needed healing from. Therefore identifying my issues wasn't so easy. Even so, reoccurring patterns in my behaviour would crop up in my relationship with Christ and others that only flared on particular occasions. Initially, I would just brush it off as nothing. However, as I started to mature in my faith, I learnt to evaluate my actions and myself constantly and be completely honest with God as well as myself.

In doing this, I realised I still had baggage from my past that I had carried over, even into my relationship with Christ. Although I had a willing heart to change, had ended toxic relationships, was filled with godly things, and knew who I was in Christ, there were still persistent, lingering, and subtle mannerisms and thoughts I was exhibiting in new relationships carried over from old ones. Self-evaluation is critical in realising the areas that still need to be worked on, and so is sensitivity to the voice of God, who also reveals these things to you (Psalm 32: 8-9, Jeremiah 33:3, John 5:30.)

I'm going to share with you the main areas in my life that God has healed/continues to heal me from. You may relate to some of them or none of them. Regardless, I hope that my own openness and transparency will help you to be open up and be honest with yourself in identifying areas in your life that are desperate for healing.

Healing from my fear of healing:

I used to be a 'bury your head in the sand type of chick.' It was my coping mechanism. I was oblivious to whatever it was I wanted to be. I had selective hearing, selective sight, and selective memory. I saw what I wanted to see, heard what I wanted to hear, and remembered what I wanted to remember. A situation would occur, and in my mind it hadn't happened simply because I didn't want it to (*True story; a guy broke up with me – very obviously, might I add, and 11 months later, I thought we had spent the last 11 months trying to make it work!*).

I would be sitting in my room or in a toilet cubicle, telling myself I was fine while crying my eyes out or self-harming. I was nearly gang raped but laughed it off minutes later (*even though it was one of the scariest situations I've been in*) to downplay the severity of what nearly happened. So when the Holy Spirit would make something plain to me that I needed restoration from, I would be like, *"Spirit, you is offff today....like waaay off!"* because I was oblivious even to my need for healing.

Can I be totally honest? I found comfort in being a victim (*I'm not trying to downplay the fact that at times I was one, but I definitely played on it*). As I started off this section by saying, I saw what I wanted to see, heard what I wanted to hear, and remembered what I wanted to remember. So when it didn't suit me to be a victim (*like when I was trying to fool myself and those around me*), I wasn't one. But when being a victim was 'useful' in certain situations (*for example, having excuses for my nasty attitude, justifying always being angry, bullying others, and treating men like absolute crap*), then all hail Christina the victim. As far as I was concerned, I was blameless in every situation, and all my hardship was everyone else's fault but mine.

When I was younger, I ashamedly used to steal money from my mum's purse, and whenever I got caught, I would blame it on not having my biological dad around (*you best believe I wasn't even using that money to 'find him.' I don't even think that man crossed my mind once – I was using the money to buy sweets and take my friends out!*). It sound silly now, but I hope this paints a vivid picture of the point I'm making. I didn't want to be healed because I liked having something/someone to blame the 'unfairness' of this world on. If Christina BC (before Christ) made an appearance AC (after Christ) in a state of anger, I didn't want to have to take full responsibility for my actions and instead looked for ways in justifying my behaviour. I would tell people that I was saved, but my past had made me an extremely defensive person, so that was the reason I had cussed out their entire existence and their generations to come. It was never because I was just a rude chick with a sharp mouth.

This means that anyone who belongs to Christ has become a new person. The old life is gone; a new life has begun! – 2 Corinthians 5:17

The moment we give our life to Christ, we are no longer victims but victors because our identity is found in Him, and our Saviour ain't no victim (halleluiah!). Yet sometimes we find comfort in calling ourselves one to justify our 'not of Christ attitude' in our 'definitely with Christ walk' that we still try to cling onto.

When you, for whatever reason, refuse to accept the healing offered to you by the Holy Spirit (Isaiah 53:4-5), you are holding unto the very past that you have been stripped of. God has given you a new identity in Him, but you're still holding on to something from your old identity in the world. As Christians, we are meant to mature in our walk (1 Corinthians 3:2); therefore, not only should we be acting differently, but our thought process should also be renewed (Romans 12:2).

In order to follow Christ wholeheartedly, we must die to ourselves daily (Luke 9:23). But every time we die to ourselves, we need God to flow in those vacant areas in our lives. Sometimes a denial of needing healing or the refusal to be healed stops God from flowing in **all** areas of our lives. And then we wonder why 10 *'I've been a Christian'* years later, we still have certain attitudes lingering within us that we just can't seem to shake.

I *used* to be a 'bury your head in the sand' sort of chick, but that was who I was *BEFORE* Christ. I understand now that I am a new person, and I take responsibility for my actions. Neither my past nor other people are to blame for how I act today because I am no longer that person that used to be bound by them. Christ really has set me free. He set me free the moment I gave my life back to Him, but it just took me a while to realise it.

Healing from my constant need for attention:

We live in a generation in which selfies are the norm, social media is the standard, and privacy seems non-existent, so it's hard to notice whether you have a constant need for attention or are simply just evolving as the world goes round.

My constant need for attention, however, was none of the above. I think I was about 7 or 8 years old when I had invasive surgery on one of my organs and spent quite a few days in Hospital recovering. In all honestly, I felt better from the operation a few days later, but do you think I was going to tell that to all the nurses and doctors who kept fussing over me? Do you think I was going to tell my mum, who was constantly at my bedside that? Or my siblings who were being extra nice to me that? No Way! Lord knows I dragged that situation out until I found the next thing to get me attention. I was kept in hospital much longer than I needed to be, and whenever the doctors or nurses asked how I was doing, it was never *"well."* I recall a doctor telling me that I would be released from hospital soon (*that's what he thought*), so I pulled out one of the tubes inserted in my lower stomach to delay that from happening (*don't know if it actually worked or not*). I craved attention so much I was even willing to hurt myself. I craved attention because I didn't feel like I got it on a day-to-day basis, so when I did get it, I was like, 'Whooooaaaaah what is this?! I love it!!!'

As I grew older and my body developed, I realised that I didn't need 'persistent stomach issues' to get attention; I could get it from the choice of clothing I wore. I could get it from a career where attention was expected, so I turned my sights on becoming a singer (*no, I can't sing – like at all!*), but was spurred on by all the people I thought would adore me once I became famous and all the people I would show off to once I was 'in the money.'

Years later, with my singing career down the drain (*thank you family members and Stars In Your Eyes*), I got saved, and not long after, God put in my heart to write this book. After doing the whole shebang of, *"Me Lord?" "You sure, Lord?" "But who am I, Lord?,"* I finally jumped on board. I wish I could say I felt then how I do now – genuinely having a desire to help others, a deep passion to share God's word, and just wanting to be so sold out for Jesus that I don't care what people think of me. I wish I could say that all I wanted to do was serve and honour my King in any way He directed me to. But 2 years ago, that was far from the truth. My initial thoughts were,

"OMG all the people that will look up to me...and for sharing God's word – the fan's....I mean, followers...I mean.... who cares what I mean! Whoever they are, they're all going to adore moi! And I'll still rub people's noses in it, and I'll still make my exes feel like leaving me was their biggest mistake like EVER! And I'll make my mum super proud, and I'll buy this and do that..." I don't even know why God saw me as someone who could make an impact when I was so focussed on the attention instead.

<u>"Watch out! Don't do your good deeds publicly, to be admired by others, for you will lose the reward from your Father in heaven. When you give to someone in need, don't do as the hypocrites do—blowing trumpets in the synagogues and streets to call attention to their acts of charity! I tell you the truth, they have received all the reward they will ever get. But when you give to someone in need, don't let your left hand know what your right hand is doing. Give your gifts in private, and your Father, who sees everything, will reward you.</u> –
Matthew 6: 1-4

As Christians; daily we say we want to be more like Jesus, but Jesus never sought attention. There were times He would perform great miracles like healing the sick, but then tell them not to tell others what He had done (Mark 1: 31-42, Mark 7:36, Matthew 9:20, Mark 5:43). Why? Maybe because in those moments He knew it was not about Him?

People hate to hear advice like what I'm just about to give because it means they too have a part to play when they would rather just sit back through all of it. But the truth is, the more time we spend with God, the more we will realise that we always had our Father's attention. You can garner all the attention in the world, but it will always be short-lived. Yet the attention given to you by God is everlasting (Luke 12:8-34.) You don't need to fight for His attention, do good deeds, be on your best behaviour, play the victim, or do anything outrageous. Even though our Father is the Father of many, He always makes us feel like he is the Father of just one – YOU! You can only lack something you don't have, and know that in Him you have everything.

I don't know about you; but for me, I genuinely no longer want it to be about 'me', because the truth is it's not, and it will never be. If people happen to look up and see me, I want them to see the God in me first.

Healing from Trust Issues:

I already shared with you in the last chapter of learning to trust God, and I'm not repeating myself, but to remain completely transparent, before I finally learnt to trust God, trusting Him was hard because I felt like He had let me down in the past *(just keep reading before you label me blasphemous!)*

For as long as I can remember (and for obvious reasons), I've always had major trust issues. Life lessons have taught me to be independent, to take care of myself, to not rely on anyone for anything, and to get myself to the top (whatever that means). So when I gave my life to Christ, trusting Him for my daily bread was hard. I read the same stories in the Bible you've probably read or heard about, and I learnt that the same

God then was the same God today. I understood that while man may fail me, God never does, and from the beginning of time, He has always remained faithful to His promises. Yet there would be occasions when I desperately wanted something to happen – like get a job, or a man. There were also times when I desperately wanted something not to happen – like my car breaking down as I drove it across the country even though I knew it was in dire need of a mechanic! I would be praying for these things, amongst others, and they never came to pass.

I knew God was dependable and trustworthy; I had experienced this for myself, but I began to feel let down by Him when certain things that I wanted didn't come to pass. I began to wrongly think, *"Maybe I'm not Christian enough,"* so I would do all the 'good deeds' I could, and when prayers still weren't answered, I would be like, *"J! We cool or……nah?"* The truth is, I never even gave God a chance to come through for me. I would only pay my tithes when I knew I would still have a substantial amount of money left over and would only pray about something when I had tried all other options and praying was my last resort – my *'just in case God decides to come through'* option. Yet I couldn't understand what I was doing wrong and tried many times to figure out God's rhyme and reason. *"The last answered prayer – I'm pretty sure I was fasting during that period....guess I'll be fasting from tomorrow, then!"* But the truth is, one of two things I was doing wrong was relying on something I thought God had promised me that He never did, (the second being never fully trusting God in the first place.)

I would hear other people's testimonies, and I would be like, *"Yep, God, me next"* without having the slightest idea of the background behind it. I just wanted the miracle. I would look for 'please me' Bible scriptures and take them straight out of context by saying things like, *"God, can you see why it's hard for me to trust You? You said that if I ask anything, You will hear me. So why have I not been heard?"* (Completely disregarding the fact that the scripture and many like it also state "according to His will.") I was allowing what I thought was God's unfaithfulness in my life to rob me of the comfort of His dependability simply because I was praying for things God did want for me, or at least not want for me in the moment I was praying for them.

The New Testament is filled with many great things that Jesus did, but there's this verse that whenever I come across it, it completely humbles me:

He went on a little farther and bowed with his face to the ground, praying, "My Father! If it is possible, let this cup of suffering be taken away from me. Yet I want your will to be done, not mine." – Matthew 26:39

Yep, even Jesus had to endure things He didn't particularly want to. He understood that everything we do should be in accordance with God's will, no matter how uncomfortable it makes us feel. Jesus is the example we all must follow.

We can't have a firm belief in what we want God to do for us (even if it is based on what He has done for others) if it's not according to His will. It's not because God doesn't love us as much. It's not because our Church were prayer and fasting for 21 days, and we only held on for 9 or because we didn't forward on a message that told us God would answer our prayers in 24 hours if we passed it on to 10 people or more. It's because what we want from God is either not what God wants for us, or not what He wants for us *yet*. Be assured, confident, free from suspicion and doubt, and have absolute faith in the fact that when you pray according to God's will, His will shall be done. What's even better is that God's will is perfect, so it's in your best interest to pray in line with His desires and not your own. (Psalm 18:30, Jeremiah 29:11, John 9:31, 1 John 2:17)

Healing from hating men:

The first man I have ever loved was my foster dad John. I remember growing up; all I ever wanted was a husband just like my daddy. I was definitely a daddy's girl and would spend hours in his shed just before tea time, watching him sand down wood or hammer nails into more wood (he's a carpenter). He always used to encourage me to write and was actually interested in hearing whatever poem or play I had just conjured up hours before. I remember him always having a packet of Werther's Original's in the back pocket of his denim, washed-out jeans (that explains why they are my favourite sweets!) And I will never forget him looking aimlessly around for a pencil even though he always had one sitting comfortably behind his ear.

It's definitely true, however, that you can have multiple good experiences in life but that one bad experience will always stick out to you. Even though I had all these fond memories of my daddy growing up which should have been the foundation of how I viewed men, I quickly forgot this when I moved back to London and watched another man dominate and emasculate my mother and keep her away from her children (just to be clear, I am not referring to my step-dad.) When I experienced a male adult, a friend of the family, sexually abuse me when I just a kid, I quickly forgot that I had ever loved a man and grew only to despise them. When a complete stranger hit me repeatedly until I 'allowed' him to force himself on me, my anger toward all men only intensified. When the most random dude ever kicked me when I was down and started spreading false rumours about us doing things I didn't even know the human body could do, there were no words on earth to describe how I felt about men. A few heartbroken relationships along the way didn't help matters either. So I went from a girl who was obsessed with her daddy and wanted a husband just like him to a bitter, hardened man-hater who would use and abuse guys as a way of 'settling the score' even though the only mistake some guys ever made towards me was showing an interest.

I entertained relationships because I hated being alone, but I was very distant in them. I became very unaffectionate, and all that lovey dovey stuff was a chore and stopped being natural for me. I actually hated guys touching me. I found it to be so gross. As far as I was concerned, all guys were slime balls, cheats, and game players. All I could remember were the negative experiences I had with guys, so I never had anything positive to say about them or to them.

After getting over my desperation of wanting to get married, I was minding my own business in the Lord and not even looking for a dude, (*but of course, some still made it through the net.*) I'm very standoffish when it comes to guys anyway (*unless I've vetted you over a long period of time and we've become strictly friends*), so I would naturally be unapproachable to these dudes that made it through the net. But after a while, I would start to think, *"Hmmmm maybe I should give him a try...I mean, he's Christian...He's still showing interest even though I'm blatantly rude and off with him.........He's a nice guy.....* But then he would do one thing (that's all it took with me) – and it could be a really silly thing like take what I considered too long to respond to a message or not call when he said he would – and that was it: He was deleted and blocked from both my phone and my heart. I would tell myself I was right all along: *'all guys are slime balls, all guys are cheats, all guys are game players'* (and a lot more explicit stuff I thought all guys were.) I was back to, *"I hate all men;" "I don't ever want to get married because it's just a way for another guy to treat me like crap...and for life! Never that!*

Over time, God has pierced through my ice-cold heart and has strategically placed some great men of God in my life that definitely sway my opinion when it comes to the opposite sex. I have great male friends in my life, pastors in my church, my daddy on earth, and my bestie in heaven who all reinforce the truth that there are great men on this earth. But if I can be completely honest: I'm not there yet. I've forgiven all the men who hurt me over the years, but I haven't forgotten. Anytime a guy disappoints me (because I don't expect anything less from them), I'm just indifferent, so blasé about them that it no longer even hurts.

Some of us have been to hell and back when it comes to guys (and this can be guys we've dated, father figures, randoms etc) and as much as we may not admit it; we know the guy who eventually wins us over is still going to have a hard time doing so, and that's not fair on them. Obviously you should know your worth, and not just give any scallywag the time of day. But equally, why should a great man – a man who loves God and is after His heart; a man who's going to love you like Christ loves the Church; a man who's going to help change the negative stereotype you still have of men suffer for the mistakes made by others?

If this is a problem you are facing, God will help to soften your heart but His word is clear: whether male or female, whether they are good or bad, and whether it *'feels'* right or wrong – we are instructed and commissioned to love one another just as we are loved by our loving Father. The world says you can love and hate someone/a group of people at the same time, but God says express only love always and love others even more than you love yourself.

Love each other with genuine affection, and take delight in honouring each other. – Romans 12:10

'You must love the Lord your God with all your heart, all your soul, and all your mind.' This is the first and greatest

commandment. A second is equally important: 'Love your neighbour as yourself.' – Matthew 22:37-39

So now I am giving you a new commandment: Love each other. Just as I have loved you, you should love each other. – John 13:34

Dear friends, let us continue to love one another, for love comes from God. Anyone who loves is a child of God and knows God. But anyone who does not love does not know God, for God is love. – 1 John 4: 7-8

But I say, love your enemies! Pray for those who persecute you! In that way, you will be acting as true children of your Father in heaven. For he gives his sunlight to both the evil and the good, and he sends rain on the just and the unjust alike. – Matthew 5: 44-45

Additional verses: John 15:12-13; Philippians 2:3-4; 1 John 4:11; Matthew 5:43-48; 1 Corinthians 13:13; Proverbs 10:12; 1 Peter 4: 8-9)

Healing from suffering in silence:

I'm really bad in my communication with others. I'm quite good at identifying why I am the way that I am in probably every other area of my life apart from when it comes to communication. With communication I'm either one extreme or another. I will either say exactly what's on my mind or clam up and not utter a word. I tend to say exactly what's on my mind when I'm angry, and I just blurt it out in a state of anger, whereas I clam up when I'm upset or annoyed and allow how I feel to just build up inside.

As I was in the process of writing this book – free from people bondage, free from dating random guys, and really enjoying this season – I found myself on my bed crying my eyes out in frustration. I was certain that God had told me to do a particular thing, but certain doors I needed to be opened to do that very thing were tightly shut. Months of built-up frustration went by, and I started to doubt I ever heard God. But of course, I wouldn't say that. I wouldn't tell God that I was overwhelmed with the assignment before me, and even though He promised to be with me always, I felt all alone. So I just sat on my bed crying. In the midst of my tears, the Holy Spirit said, *"Talk to me. Tell me how you feel. Tell me what's going on. Just express yourself to me."* But I didn't know how to; I hadn't reached that stage of being so angry that I blurt it out so I just went mute instead.

You are my friends if you do what I command. I no longer call you slaves, because a master doesn't confide in his slaves. Now you are my friends, since I have told you everything the Father told me. You didn't choose me. I chose you. I appointed you to go and produce lasting fruit, so that the Father will give you whatever you ask for, using my name. This is my command: Love each other. - John 15:14-17

You see, God desires a friendship with us. He wants more than just us 'occasionally' feeling His presence during prayer time; He wants companionship with us all the time. He wants us to have an intimate heart-to-heart relationship with Him, just like Abraham (James 2:23).

I've often wondered why Abraham was called a friend of God (2 Chronicles 20:7; Isaiah 41:8; James 2:23). Moses, another great man in the Old Testament was often referred to as a servant of God (Joshua 1:1; 1 Chronicles 6:49; Daniel 9:11). Yet Abraham was repeatedly referred as God's friend. One thing that stands out to me is that Abraham was a man of tremendous faith:

It was by faith that Abraham offered Isaac as a sacrifice when God was testing him. Abraham, who had received God's promises, was ready to sacrifice his only son, Isaac, even though God had told him, "Isaac is the son through whom your descendants will be counted." Abraham reasoned that if Isaac died, God was able to bring him back to life again. And in a sense, Abraham did receive his son back from the dead." – Hebrews 11:17-19

Do you ever feel like you're suffering in silence because it feels 'weird' talking out loud to God you can't see? It feels uncomfortable stepping out in faith? And it feels odd having a friendship with God? God's our Master, our King, our Father - but our friend as well? How?

I didn't have a friendship with God because I didn't have the faith to understand that I could. I couldn't confide in Him as you do a friend because, like every friendship that develops naturally, I never just communicated with Him unless I wanted something. I didn't understand that even when I failed to utter the words because my heart was too burdened or confused,

God still hears the thoughts of my heart (Romans 8:26). That's what a real friend does: They listen in whatever way you choose to express yourself. Now I converse with God all the time (*maybe a bit too much.*) We have date nights, go shopping, crack jokes (*although the jokes are always on me*), and His sense of humour is one of the things I love most about Him! I no longer suffer in silence because I have a constant friend in Jesus Christ. By having better communication with Him, I've learnt to have better communication with others. I don't have to wait until I'm angry past the point of no return to 'state my truth' to others, and I don't need to feel like I don't have a voice either.

Healing from the stereotype of singleness:

I told myself various times to stop writing this book for many different reasons. My whole business being out there was definitely one of them, but probably the most notable reason was because I didn't want to be the 'poster girl' for single chicks. As explained over the course of this book, I haven't always found joy and contentment in this season, and I didn't want to be associated with singledom for the rest of my life.

There are certain people and names that when they come to mind, you associate them with what you know them for (for example: Barack Obama – presidency/politics; Priscilla Shirer – articulate/*War Room*; Tasha Cobbs – amazing/gospel/singer; Ricky – Rickayyy/Eastenders; Patricia Bright – hair/makeup). Now, I'm not saying that I'm in the same league as any of these people or even comparing myself to them, but what I am saying is I didn't want my ministry to revolve around singleness because I thought that's all people would associate me with. I still held this negative stereotype of singleness as being undesirable, left behind, and alone, and I didn't know how I would ever complete a book encouraging other woman to love this season when at times I couldn't even encourage myself.

Oh, the joys of those who do not follow the advice of the wicked, or stand around with sinners, or join in with mockers. But they delight in the law of the Lord, meditating on it day and night. They are like trees planted along the riverbank, bearing fruit each season. Their leaves never wither and they prosper in all they do. – Psalm 1:1-3

Sis, I hope you realise that there truly is beauty in every season we find ourselves in, and it brings joy to the Lord to produce a harvest in each and every one of those seasons. Let's stop looking at our single days as a curse when it is such a blessing and one we shouldn't want to rush getting out of. We get to experience God all for ourselves without having to devote our time and attention to anyone else. We get to discover what God desires for us, and we get to heal before someone else enters our life.

This book has taken over 2 years to write, but the woman I was at the start of writing this book isn't the woman I am as this book draws to a close. I am so thankful because there's so much that I have experienced in this season that I couldn't have experienced in any other season. Let the world label me whatever they like – my focus and priority is my Father's Kingdom that lasts forever, not this dying World that daily fades away.

If you're reading this and are identifying negative traits that your still not healed from – no matter how long it's been or even how long you've been a Christian, allow God to purge you, heal you, strengthen you, work within you, and mould you (Isaiah 41:10). Don't continue to bury your head in the sand, hoping you will 'heal yourself.' Don't be naïve in thinking your insecurities, attention-seeking ways, lack of communication towards others, nit-picking behaviour and whatever else; will all just disappear away when another guy comes on the scene.

If you're single in Christian terms (i.e. not married) but not single in the social definition of the word (i.e. you do have le boo) but you still recognise areas that need healing, I'm not suggesting you break up with le boo (that is not my call to make). But I believe that even within your courting relationship, God can heal and restore you (Joel 2:25, Ephesians 2:8, Titus 3:5). However, for those who are completely single (both in the Christian and the social definition of the word), I believe you are better off being healed before a relationship then while in one.

Chapter 5

And In The Meantime...

Part 1: Why Are You Waiting?

As already explained in the last chapter, I think it's so important to heal first before entering new relationships. But while we heal, I don't believe in just 'waiting' around for a spouse.

I've been single for over 6 years now, and while this season hasn't always been a bed of blossoming roses, keeping myself busy in the Lord definitely has made this season a lot easier. In my single years before I came to Christ, I was a jumper – jumping from one relationship to another and waiting to meet my prince charming in the midst of kissing frogs (*no offence to my exes.*) After I got saved and God showed me that I was doing dissatisfaction to myself in just waiting, I got busy in the Lord. I spent hours with Him, getting to know Him and fellowshipping with Him. I got involved in various volunteering work – from pre-teens to the elderly. I became more involved in my church, I travelled on my own; I have become a point of contact to young woman struggling with various issues ranging from promiscuity to understanding who God is. I took a job that allows me to travel often overseas (*which I would have never taken If I was in a relationship.*) I wrote this book, I'm developing a screenplay and I'm also involved in a candy business with my friend.

I've done all these things simultaneously that I doubt I would have ever been open to or would have had the time to do if I was married. I can't believe I would have missed out on all these great opportunities just because I was waiting around for the man of my dreams. Meanwhile, the man of my dreams is living his life and enjoying this season while God is preparing him for me!

It is true that in the well-known biblical story of Ruth and Boaz, Ruth was working (keeping busy) when Boaz noticed her (Ruth 2:2-7), but it is also true that Ruth was in a position to get married when Boaz made clear his intentions (Ruth 4). While you are just sitting around waiting for le boo, how does that prepare you for when le boo finally arrives?

Let me tell you the issue of '*waiting for a man*' by using the following illustration:

I'm on my way to work, I've checked my bus app, and it shows the next bus coming in 5 minutes. No problem – I'll leave my house in 2 minutes (the bus stop is literally downstairs from my flat.) Seven minutes later; I'm chilling at the bus stop, and there's still no bus in sight. I've refreshed my bus app once again, and all it shows is the bus being due. I begin to grow inpatient. I check my messages to waste time. I hear a bus come and look up with a '*finally*' sigh only to see it's a bus on the opposite site of the road going in another direction. I wait a few more minutes, then, even though I hate changing buses, I consider taking 2 different buses, which takes 15 minutes longer to my destination. Now I'm agitated. When my bus finally arrives 14 minutes later, I'm so peed off that the bus driver doesn't get a thank you from me, and I moan about it to my work colleagues at least until midday!

When we wait for a spouse, we grow agitated and restless because we're not doing anything else (even though God ordained work for man and detests laziness: Proverbs 10:4; Proverbs 6: 9-11; Proverbs 12:24). We grow weary and keep ourselves busy doing nothing to make the time pass more quickly. We consider substitutes for what we really want because that now seems like an easier option. Then when a guy finally comes along, we're ungrateful because although he finally arrived, he still was 'late.' We complain to God, our peers, and our family that we wasted all this time waiting for this dude, and now that he's finally here, we're disappointed with what we've now got.

I get it; you're burdened wondering where you are going to meet him. All the good men are taken, there are no Christian men at work, there are no good looking ones at church, and there are none you like at the social gatherings you attend, but so what? During the 40 years the Israelites wondered around the wilderness, they faced really tough conditions, including a scarcity of food. However, God still miraculously provided for their needs by providing manna each morning. Manna is known as 'bread from heaven' (Exodus 16: 4-15). So why do you then doubt the same God to provide you with exactly what you need when you need it? God Himself says:

Seek the Kingdom of God above all else, and he will give you everything you need – Luke 12: 31

So trust in His faithfulness that has led you this far.

During the healing process and through the single season; even though we're **not** waiting on a man and are busy in the Lord, let's not live our lives with this warped fantasy of a guy either.

There was this guy that I used to like – *yes, Christina – Ice Queen, Leader Of The Standoffish Crew; Ms. Single for 6 years and Counting* – liked a dude. (I know!) But this dude was (from what I could see, anyway) a righteous man of God, very involved in his church, handsome, and he gave off this vibe that he liked me. Anyway, I had only seen this guy in social settings, so I never had one-on-one time with him – *yes, Christina – Follower of the 'Be Busy in Christ Movement; Righteous Woman of God, Head of 'Virtuous & Hidden in Christ' Committee* – wanted-one-on-one time with this dude. (I know!) So as I waited for one-on-one time with this dude, I had this fantasy of what it would be like. I imagined that he would sweep me off my feet. We would spend hours on the phone in prayer and discussing the Bible. I dreamed of the moment he would meet my foster dad before asking for my soft & slender hand in marriage. I thought about whether I would attend his church or convince him to come to mine after we became husband and wife. I had concluded that his surname with my first name did not have a nice ring to it – but hey, that's marriage – you compromise.

Months later, I finally get one-on-one time with this guy, and it was nothing – and I do mean *not* even close to what I had imagined. I then got angry – this dude led me on (*meanwhile, he never led me anywhere*). I felt like all guys are the same – they lie, they cheat, they're game players. I blocked and deleted him from both my phone and heart. And when I happened to run into him, he got the cold shoulder. While this guy is thinking, *'Ok, this chick is super weird,'* I'm nursing an upset heart all because of this fantasy I created in my head of what I thought a relationship with a particular person would be like.

Marriage is beautiful, but marriage also might not be what you envisioned it being like. So don't get hurt and disappointed like me; don't walk around with this ideology and fantasy of what you expect it to be. Wait to experience it for what it really is when the time does come.

Part 2: But should we wait until marriage to have sex? YES

I would be doing an injustice to you ladies if I didn't talk about sex outside of marriage because it's something we do to ourselves that causes so much damage. I'm not condemning anyone at all (*I've been there myself);* but I want to make it clear that you hurt yourself over and over every time you choose to lay in another man's bed (or get him to lay in yours – whichever.)

Healing from past hurt and pain is important, but so is closing your legs to a man who is not your husband. I know it's uncomfortable, 'touchy,' and even a taboo subject to talk about – especially in this generation, but regardless – it needs to be said. Sexual immorality is seen and heard everywhere; it's rampant, and yet the effects it has on us as women are hardly, if at all mentioned.

Some of you have already set that boundary, and that's great. I hope this section acts a reminder to you. Yet others are thinking, '*Let me just skip through this section. I already know that as a Christian, sex outside of marriage is wrong, but I'll still do it because I like it, it's impossible not to have sex/I can't control myself/I won't get a boyfriend if I don't give it up/I really love him, I mean reeeeaaaallly L.O.V.E him/everyone else is doing it/I need to make sure the engine works before I buy the car/I need to know that we are sexually compatible/I lack intimacy with a guy without it,*' and other reasons. But even so, I can't ignore the responsibility to reiterate a few points as well as provide clarity for those who genuinely don't understand what the big fuss is about.

Yes, having sex outside of marriage can lead to an unwanted pregnancy *("but were using contraception")* or sexually transmitted infections/diseases *("but I make sure he uses a condom")*, but none of that can protect you from heartbreak experienced when it doesn't work out even after you've given him your body. You can't be sheltered from feeling cheap or used the moment you give in and he stops showing interest. How do you guard yourself from being sure that a guy is genuinely into you rather than just lusting over you? How do you safeguard yourself from the cycle of using sex as a tool to keep a guy interested? How do you mend the relationship when you notice a disconnect and sex won't repair it even though it has always worked before? How do you protect yourself from the insecurity and panic you experience when you need to be away from your dude for a while and know he can't go 3 days without it? And most importantly, how do you protect yourself from the separation of God's presence because you are living in habitual sin?

I could throw at you a ton of scriptures to keep yourself pure, like:

"*Marriage should be honoured by everyone, and husband and wife should keep their marriage pure. God will judge as guilty those who take part in sexual sins.*" - Hebrews 13:4

"*Flee from sexual immorality. Every other sin a person commits is outside the body, but the sexually immoral person sins against his own body. Or do you not know that your body is a temple of the Holy Spirit within you, whom you have from God? You are not your own, for you were bought with a price. So glorify God in your body.*" - 1 Corinthians 6:18-20

For this is the will of God, your sanctification: that you abstain from sexual immorality; that each one of you know how to control his own body in holiness and honour, not in the passion of lust like the Gentiles who do not know God; that no one transgress and wrong his brother in this matter, because the Lord is an avenger in all these things, as we told you beforehand and solemnly warned you. For God has not called us for impurity, but in holiness - 1 Thessalonians 4:3-8

But woman to woman, sister to sister; I really want you to understand that a few minutes of sexual gratification is not worth the lifetime of destruction you're causing yourself. That guy has not paid the price for you; therefore, you are not for sale! Why can't you see that you are worth so much more than a few minutes of pleasure?

The Son of God came to this earth and suffered just for you. He was ridiculed, beaten, and tortured all while having you in mind. He sacrificed His sinless life for your sinful one, yet **Mr. Unwilling To Wait** sacrifices nothing! If he really loves you – if you are really wife material or the queen he says you are – then why does he treat you like you have no value? Why does he defile you every night before you go to bed?

That's not the kind of love Paul spoke about when he told husbands to love their wives just as Christ loves the Church and gave himself for her (Ephesians 5:25). If he's not committed to a relationship with you without sex, then be pleasant enough to hold the door wide open for him as he exists your life, because he isn't worth it. You are not a prude or old fashioned because you have standards that are based on God's best for your life. You are a woman of God, a virtuous woman, a woman whose husband will honour her and their relationship, and a woman whose husband is going to be so in love with God that no matter what his flesh desires, he will not take something that does not yet belong to him.

Don't you understand that God loves you and you are precious to Him? He's not denying you of something that He Himself created; He's protecting you from the devastation it causes when it is done outside of His will. He knows that when you become intimate with another person, you then become <u>one flesh</u> and are bound by him physically, spiritually, and emotionally (Matthew 19:5). He created that bond for married couples – to make their relationships stronger, closer, more unique, and immeasurable to any other kind of relationships they have. Yet you are willing to create that same bond with *Mr. Non-Committed* and wonder why years later, while you lay in another man's bed, you are still thinking about another guy all because of that stronghold you both share simply because you didn't understand your worth.

Don't you desire a relationship in which you both exercise self-discipline? In which you both connect on an emotional and intellectual level because lust isn't calling the shots? When, if the relationship doesn't work out, you can both walk away unscathed because you didn't cross any boundaries? Don't you want a relationship that ministers to people who are struggling? That proves God's way is the best way and shows that purity is still present and desired in this society in which sex seems so easy to get?

It doesn't matter if you're reading this book as you lay in his bed with your head on his chest (*although I strongly suggest you carry your fine behind home*), if you and a dude have already made arrangements to do the deed soon, or if you're madly in love with him or feel bad about abruptly stopping something you already started. What matters are the consequences of living an unrighteous and sinful life because for whatever reason you refuse to just say NO. You cannot gratify your flesh while living to please God at the same time. You can only serve one master, so which one are you serving?

Just as He did with Joseph and Potiphar's wife (Genesis 39), God will always create a way out of temptation. But it will always be your choice of whether you take it or not. If this is an area that you are struggling with, then stop whatever you are doing right now and confess your sins onto the Lord. He knows your struggles and promises to forgive and cleanse you from **ALL** unrighteousness (1 John 1:9). Make a commitment today that the next and only guy you will be physical with will be your husband on your wedding night after he has made a vow before God and your loved ones to cherish you as long as you both shall live. There is always joy and favour to be experienced at the end of your obedience, so stay encouraged! (2 Peter 2:21).

To my beautiful sisters who have already made that promise to God and your future spouse: congratulations! Please remember that although you have said it with your mouth, your actions should follow. Pay attention to the way that you dress, ladies! Don't confuse these poor boys or make any room for temptation! I'm not saying that you need to be completely covered from your neck to your ankles, but when you're shopping online or at your favourite store, ask the Holy Spirit if the items of clothing are ok to buy. When you've got your outfit ready to wear or already on, before you step out of your house, get the Lord's seal of approval first. Let's be intentional about saving every bit of ourselves for our husband's eyes only (FYI, that guy who you've been courting for 2 years is not your husband – he doesn't deserve to see your assets any more than *Mr. Too Irrelevant To Even Have A Name* does.)

Set boundaries at the beginning of any relationship so there is absolutely no room for confusion for either person. If you know that a guy kissing your hand sends shivers down your spine, you better just warn him that there will be none of that until you guys are married! If going to the cinema makes you want to snuggle up, huddle up, and then touch up with your partner, then make sure you never go alone to the cinema, or don't go at all. There is nothing wrong with setting boundaries, no matter how silly they seem to be. It's actually a sign of maturity and demonstrates your commitment to a Christian courtship. Remember that courting is still part of the journey. God does not require our standards to slip just because we think were in love. Let's make our relationship with our future spouses be different from all the other relationships we've experienced.

Chapter 6

Stay Encouraged: You Got This!

Can I get an amen! *(Amen),* because I can't believe we are near the end of this incredible journey. I really hope this book has blessed you and that God has started working in your life even before you reached this page. Writing this book has made me laugh, cry, and feel uncomfortable at times. But through it all, I know God has been healing what was broken and restoring in me what was lost. Just as He's been blessing me in more ways than I can count while writing this, I pray that He blesses you also for taking the time to read it.

Even though I feel like I could write forever; I'm pretty sure I would run out of content for the other books I'm planning to write! So before I bid farewell, I just want to recap a few things mentioned throughout this book:

1) If it's been a while since you've heard these words, then let me just remind you, my incredible, beloved sister in Christ: **YOU ARE BEAUTIFUL**. I may have never met

you, but I know that you are made by a perfect God and in His perfect image, so I say this with confidence. The colour of your skin, the length or texture of your hair, that your nose is bigger or flatter compared to other noses, or your body that is straight rather than hourglass are not mistakes; you are so unique and have been created in such a special way that you are doing yourself an injustice to not embrace it.

2) YOU **HAVE PURPOSE**! God did not make a mistake in creating you, and neither has He forgotten the plans for your life. God is not the father of confusion; He will never leave you half way without finishing what He has started in your life (Philippians 1:6). So rest assured that He will grant you the desires of your heart (Psalms 37:4.) But in the meantime, make sure you are walking the path specifically designed for you and that your eyes are solely fixed on the Lord and not on what He can do for you.

3) Recognise that your worth and value come from God and not from your marital status, families and friends' opinions, or society's standards on how your life should be by a particular age. If you've gone from being a part of a group of Singletons to the last single still standing within the same group, so what? Embrace it, take advantage of not having a husband to answer to, and do the things you've always wanted to do! It doesn't matter your age right now; there is no expiry date on God's love for you. Not being married at 35 doesn't mean that you don't deserve a spouse, that you've missed your turn, or whatever lies you allow the enemy to feed you. It just means

that it isn't God's appointed time for you. His timing is perfect, so allow Him to write your love story. Surrender yourself to Him completely and trust that when the time is right, your spouse will *find* you.

4) Let us start or continue to be intentional about living a life of purity that is pleasing to the Lord. Don't cry, *'Lord, where is my Isaac?'* as you live your life like Jezebel. Live your life in a way that follows and honours God's words. Don't contradict your faith by how you act, what comes out of your mouth, or how you choose to dress. God requires us to live lives of holiness right up until the moment we depart this earth.

5) You don't need to be jealous of your friends who are already married or who are courting; be genuinely happy for them the same way you would expect them to be happy for you when your time comes. Remember: It's not called 'being jealous because my friend has a boyfriend'; it's called being jealous FULL STOP. The jealously won't go away when you get married; all that will happen is that you will find something else to be jealous of (like being jealous that your bestie is on her 4th child and you're still struggling to get pregnant with your first.)

6) Understand that it hurts your Heavenly Father when He sees you make yet another random guy your idol, when you relentlessly keep chasing *Mr. Non Committed, Mr. Manipulator,* and *Mr. Compulsive Liar* when He's preparing *Mr. Will Love You Like Christ Loves The Church* just for you!

7) And how do you deal with the possibility that you may never get married? God loves you; you are cherished by Him and protected by Him. So with confidence, I say that God would never place a desire on your heart He had no intention of bringing to pass. If you also believe this and know God has placed in you the desire for a spouse, it's not a matter of *if* but **when**. Of course, God calls some people not to marry (1 Corinthians 7:1-40); however, in these situations, God will make it clear that this is not His will over your life. Being single or married is a gift from God; therefore, God will equip you to handle either.

8) God will hold us all *individually* accountable one day – not as husband and wife, for Jesus makes it clear that there is no marriage in heaven (Matthew 22:30). Can you afford to stand in front of God and tell Him you didn't fulfill your purpose, and souls you were destined to save are not saved, all as a result of you not getting married?

SHOUT OUT TO MY FELLOW SINGELTON'S: Whether you are the *'Single Mother'*; the *'Divorcee;'* the *'Single & Miserable'*; the *'Single For So Long'*; the *'45-Year-Old'* single; the *'Pretend I Don't Care'* single; the *'Promiscuous'* single; the *'If I Don't Meet Bae At This Event'* single; The *'I Trust God'* single; the *'Happy & Content'* single; the *'I Can't believe I'm Still Single'* single; the *'Struggling To Trust God'* single; the *'Nearly Was Married'* Single or the *'Single Christian'*: Never forget that delay is not denial. Just because you don't see le boo in your life, that doesn't mean he's not on his way (Genesis 16:1-6; 2 Peter 3:9.)

Let us all draw a close of messing around with *Mr. Player Player, Mr. Compulsive Liar,* and *Mr. Non Committed* When **Mr. Till Death Do Us Part, Mr. Loves you like Christ Loves The Church**, and **Mr. Indescribable** are your portion and waiting on the other side of your obedience?

So stay encouraged, sis: You got this!